JULIAN *of* NORWICH

JULIAN *of* NORWICH

A very brief history

JANINA RAMIREZ

First published in Great Britain in 2016

Society for Promoting Christian Knowledge
36 Causton Street
London SW1P 4ST
www.spck.org.uk

Paperback edition published 2017

British Library Cataloguing-in-Publication Data
A catalogue record for this book is available from the British Library

ISBN 978–0–281–07737–3 (hardback)
ISBN 978–0–281–07684–0 (paperback)
eBook ISBN 978–0–281–07685–7

Typeset by Graphicraft Limited, Hong Kong
First printed in Great Britain by TJ International
Subsequently digitally printed in Great Britain by Ashford Colour Press

eBook by Graphicraft Limited, Hong Kong

Produced on paper from sustainable forests

994440884

To Uncle Zbyszek, who lit the touch paper,
Vincent Gillespie, who fanned the flames,
Jane Hawkes and Mary Garrison,
who curbed the wild fire,
and my colleagues and students at Oxford
University, who light fires of their own.

And to those I love.

'They who love most shall be most blessed,
not they who lead the most austere life,
for love outweigheth this.'
Ancrene Wisse: Guide for Anchoresses

Contents

Preface   ix

Chronology   xiii

Part 1
THE HISTORY

1 Introducing Julian   3

2 Julian's life and times   17

3 Themes in *Revelations of Divine Love*   37

Part 2
THE LEGACY

4 A brief history of *Revelations of Divine Love*   73

Notes   86

Further reading   89

Index   93

Preface

Revelations of Divine Love is a strange book to read. It is the earliest surviving book written by a woman in English. And it is strange because it is too complex a work simply to read through cover-to-cover. It contains the contemplations of one mind across decades, thoughts that the enigmatic Julian of Norwich returned to again and again while walled up, living out her death as an anchoress within the four walls of her cell. There are coherent threads, but it ranges widely and draws its strands together like a spider's web. I first read it as a complete work, yet it left me wanting to go back and dissect it, scrutinize certain passages and read sections out of sequence. A recent translator on the text commented that 'Julian needs to be taken in short measures, not downed by the pint', and I would agree.[1] Of all the works I have read, hers is the one I most want to read passage by passage, phrase by phrase, word by word. As she gave time to writing it, we must give time to reading it. The rewards are immense.

Her very name, Julian of Norwich, reflects the enigmatic mix of mystery and reality combined in this incredibly important woman: the first known woman to write in English. Her name has become synonymous with the place in which she was walled up as an anchoress for up to thirty years – the Church of St Julian in Norwich. But apart from this basic information, we know very little about Julian herself. A woman in a man's world, her name reveals a patriarchal Church where women had to navigate a thorny path if they wanted their voices to be heard. Scholarship, spirituality, study – these were the preserve of men rather than women, so for a woman to write a book in the fourteenth century was both dangerous and difficult.

But what a book she wrote. Her *Revelations of Divine Love* offers timeless insights into God, love, sin, suffering, all in a form of poetic prose that is unique, beautiful and powerfully moving – in English. The book and the name of its author were nearly lost to the fires of reformers and the passage of time, but over six centuries a sequence of female thinkers protected their memory, so that, against the odds, her voice can still be heard today. Julian deserves to be seen as the female Chaucer or the female Thomas More. But her femininity is not the only thing to define her. *Revelations of Divine Love* would be considered an exceptional book written at any time or place, written by a man or a woman. The fact that it was written by a female anchorite, in fourteenth-century Norwich, at a turbulent and religiously significant time, makes it all the more fascinating.

The book Julian wrote contains passages that have given hope to many during times of pain or suffering. It is a book full of positivity and optimism, but it also contains ideas about spirituality that continue to resonate in our modern world. When describing the universe as a hazelnut that she holds in her hands, Julian is expressing an idea of enlightenment that underlies all world religions, and is the goal of so many spiritual seekers today. When contemplating God's love as that of a mother, she can appeal to modern readers searching for a religious view that draws on both the male and female. When describing love and peace as all that matters, she shows a spiritual path that chimes with current feelings against war and hostility. When she says 'all shall be well', many of us today want to hear that.

Julian deserves to be better known. As Mother of English literature, she deserves recognition, but the quality of her work, the potency of her prose, the beauty of the revelations and the broad-minded way in which she engages with Christian ideas, all mean she rewards a lifetime of study. Excellent modern translations of Julian's text are now readily available, and new research is continually appearing to shed more light on her. Pope Francis recently cited her, drawing inspiration from this medieval anchorite from Norwich, stating: 'In one of her visions, Julian of Norwich hears the Lord say that he rejoices eternally because he was able to suffer for our sake out of love.'[2] The Queen has 'all shall be well, all shall be well, and all manner of things shall be well' on a stained glass window in front of her when she prays at the Chapel Royal in St James's Palace. Julian's importance is recognized, but we should be celebrating her more. This little book is my small contribution.

I want to thank everyone who helped with the writing of this book. Philip Law and SPCK have been wonderfully supportive at every stage, as have Rosemary Scoular, Aoife Rice and Ed Hodgson. The Bodleian Library, as always, supplied all the research materials I could have hoped for and more. The sisters at Stanbrook Abbey, Yorkshire, particularly Sister Scholastica and Abbess Andrea, gave tirelessly of their knowledge and archives to assist with tracing the legacy of Julian. Fabian Laforge at the Municipal Library in Cambrai provided access to the catalogue of the convent's holdings, and both the British Library, London and the Bibliothèque Nationale in Paris allowed me access to the two earliest surviving manuscripts of *Revelations of Divine Love*. The British Museum has also assisted in terms of access to the fourteenth-century crucifix, and Norwich Cathedral similarly with the Despenser Retable.

There are many people striving to get Julian's story out to a wider audience: Sally-Ann Lomas, Margit Thofner, Richard Graveling, Steve Absomb and all at Tin Can Island. My thanks go out to the Bishop of Norwich and to Rowan Williams for making time to discuss Julian with me. Of course, this book would not have been written without the love and support of my family. Dan, Kuba and Kama, Babi and Papa, you all know that love is the meaning. My greatest thanks are reserved for Professor Vincent Gillespie. I would never have known of Julian, or indeed continued my lifelong passion for medieval literature, if he had not ignited a spark in my undergraduate years. His devotion to Julian has remained strong for decades, and I hope this short introduction will encourage more people to see how one woman's work, written over six hundred years ago, can reward a lifetime of study.

Chronology

1300   Birth of Richard Rolle

1303   Birth of Bridget of Sweden, famous mystic

1309   Pope Clement V moves the papacy to Avignon

1320   Birth of John Wycliffe

1327   Death of Edward II and beginning of the reign of Edward III

1337   Start of the Hundred Years War with France

1340   Birth of Walter Hilton, author of *The Scale of Perfection*

1343   Birth of Julian of Norwich and Geoffrey Chaucer

1349   The Black Death reaches England

1370   Henry Despenser becomes Bishop of Norwich

1373   Birth of Margery Kempe and date Julian receives her revelations

1378   Pope Gregory XI moves the papacy back to Rome. Start of the Great Western Schism

1381   The Peasants' Revolt. Chancellor Simon Sudbury is killed
The Battle of North Walsham, where Despenser defeats Geoffrey Litster

1382   The Earthquake Synod, which ruled on the works of John Wycliffe

1383   Henry Despenser leads the Norwich men on crusade

1390   Julian has taken anchoritic vows and entered the cell at the Church of St Julian

1395   Rough date when Julian begins writing *Revelations of Divine Love*

Chronology

1401 *De Haeretico Comburendo* passed, which punished heretics with burning at the stake

1413 Margery Kempe visits Julian

1416 Death of Julian of Norwich

1606 Birth of Gertrude More

1625 English Benedictine nuns found the monastery at Cambrai, France

1670 Serenus de Crecy publishes printed version of *Revelations of Divine Love*

1789 Start of the French Revolution

1793 Cambrai nuns are expelled from France

1877 Henry Collins publishes printed version of *Revelations of Divine Love*

1901 Grace Warrack publishes *Revelations* through Methuen, which becomes widely popular

2001 Julian's words are included in the Queen's Jubilee window at St James's Palace

Part 1

THE HISTORY

1

Introducing Julian

Revelations of Divine Love is not an autobiography, in that it contains virtually no details about the life and times of its author. Julian is remarkably absent from her text. We learn nothing about her childhood, whether she had a family, where she lived, what occupied her outside prayer and contemplation. However, it is a spiritual autobiography, charting the inner journey of Julian's mind and soul following a set of sixteen revelations that she received at the age of thirty. It charts her constant struggle to engage with the big questions of life: Who is God? How should we know him? Does sin exist? How can we survive in a life full of pain and suffering? What is the purpose of my life on earth? In this respect her text exists outside its time, and can be as relevant, comforting and thought-provoking now as it was in the fourteenth century.

'Julian of Norwich's day was a long time coming.'[1] All commentators on Julian's *Revelations of Divine Love* agree that her work has stayed in the shadows for too long. When it first appeared in print some three hundred years after it was written, it received the harshest of reviews. Bishop Stillingfleet declared it the 'fantastic revelations of a distempered brain'. Written in Middle English, containing mystical visions gleaned through meditation upon a gory gothic image of Christ, and steeped in Catholic medieval ideas, Julian's text fared poorly in post-Reformation England.

As monasteries were dismantled and images attacked, so texts such as the *Revelations of Divine Love* were destroyed, scorned and driven underground. Yet it found a way to survive down the centuries, largely through the dedication of a sequence of intellectual, strong and determined women. That we even have Julian's text today is little short of a miracle, and despite being a long time coming, her day is now.

One issue readers of Julian's text can encounter, whether they read the original or a sensitive translation, is that she wrote in Middle English. Her dialect, East Anglian, is not as complicated to read as some other fourteenth-century texts, but it can still be startling for a modern reader. Some words appear recognizable, for example 'behovely', and yet their meaning can be complex and rooted specifically in the time and place in which they were written. Reading Julian out loud in the original can be a good way to hear the meaning of her phrases. It also allows the beauty of her prose to be truly effective. The pronunciation of her vowels is slightly longer and higher than our modern equivalents, and closer to a broad northern accent than a modern Norwich one.

Her text survives in two versions, known as the 'Short Text' and the 'Long Text'. The first may have been written as early as 1388, shortly after Julian had her revelations, while the longer version, which contains an expanded and more sophisticated set of ruminations on her visions, could have been recorded late in her life. The Short Text survives in a single copy, made in the fifteenth century, and it has an immediacy and spontaneity to it that may indicate it was recorded from recent memory. The Long Text shows a greater degree of authorial consciousness, and the theology is far more developed, which may indicate that it has been worked and reworked over a number of years. It is remarkable that we have both versions surviving. Whatever the timings of the Short and Long Texts, to have two different accounts of Julian's *Revelations of Divine Love* suggests that the little historical information we have about Julian's life is borne out by the manuscripts; she had her visions, became an anchoress, lived for a long time afterwards, and continually returned to her revelations as she ruminated on them day after day, year after year.

All Julian wants us to know about her she includes in her text. She was born around 1343, received her visions at the age of 30 in 1373, and was still alive in 1416. She had many years to develop her understanding of what was shown to her over a period of three days and nights as she lay dying. To understand fully what she believed were 'divine shewings', she took the seemingly drastic step of being enclosed as an anchoress inside a cell, which was probably to the north side of the Church of St Julian, on King Street in Norwich. Becoming an anchoress around the age of 43, she lived on for up to thirty years in one room, her only door to the world walled up, and her enclosure confirmed by the last rites. This saw her as effectively dead to this world. In watching her own last rites she was a witness at her own funeral, and her existence within the cell was akin to living within a tomb.

Medieval mysticism

The text that she produced while locked within her cell is best described as 'medieval mysticism'. All major world religions have a mystical element, and it can be understood as 'a personal, unmediated approach to, and attainment of, a direct apprehension of God' (*Oxford English Dictionary*).

By the fourteenth century, when Julian wrote *Revelations of Divine Love*, the mystical tradition was gathering momentum across Europe and becoming extremely popular. Hildegard of Bingen was one of the first female mystics to establish the tradition. She was a remarkable woman, who in the twelfth century experienced visions but who was also renowned for her work in medicine, music, poetry, natural history, philosophy, mathematics and linguistics. She was a nun and abbess, but as the centuries progressed, women outside convents began to experience, publicize and record visions, and priests became fascinated with them.

Mystical texts became very popular and circulated widely. Marie of Oignies was heralded as a visionary, despite being a laywoman, and she was afflicted with uncontrollable tears and ecstasies. She wore only white, ate no meat and mortified her flesh, traits that English mystics such as Margery Kempe would later assume in emulation of a medieval celebrity. One of the most famous mystics of the fourteenth century was St Bridget of Sweden, now one of the six patron saints of Europe. Like Julian, she received revelations, though hers started at the age of ten. She too saw an image of the crucifix and interacted with Christ. Extremely popular in her lifetime, her writings were later widely condemned, Martin Luther declaring her *die tolle Brigit* ('the crazy Bridget'),[2] and William Marshall, the sixteenth-century English Protestant Reformer, encouraging people to 'forget such prayers as those of Saint Bridget'.[3]

Mystical texts have often been scorned, since they rarely follow the tone and approach of traditional religious works, encouraging instead an immediate and intimate understanding of the divine. As a result, the online *Oxford English Dictionary* also includes this definition of 'mysticism':

Freq. *derogatory*. Religious belief that is characterized by vague, obscure, or confused spirituality; a belief system based on the assumption of occult forces, mysterious supernatural agencies, etc.

Despite the scepticism with which mystical texts could be viewed, they were incredibly popular in the medieval period. They present, often in beautiful and expressive language, an experience or set of experiences that have allowed an author to move beyond the limits of normal human thought, into an area that is inexplicable and based on feelings or sensations. For mystical writers, knowledge – the preserve of the few – was not academic, but experiential. Because Julian of Norwich and her fellow English mystics were writing within a fourteenth-century Christian framework, they call the divine 'God' and understand their experiences through Christian theology. Yet moving beyond the problems of human existence to a greater understanding of how these problems can be transformed is not limited to Christian readers. *Revelations of Divine Love* is a book in which people of all religions and backgrounds can find solace and inspiration. Blake tapped into the universal feeling of transcendence that the mystic experiences when he wrote:

> To see a World in a Grain of Sand
> And a Heaven in a Wild Flower,
> Hold Infinity in the palm of your hand
> And Eternity in an hour.[4]

There are five well-known English mystics, who all lived roughly contemporaneously: Walter Hilton, Richard Rolle, the anonymous author of *The Cloud of Unknowing*, Margery Kempe and Julian. All chose to write not in Latin, the language of the Church, but in English. This may be because the sensory, visceral experiences they recount depend on the spoken vernacular for potency.[5] The inexplicable is best described in one's mother tongue, rather than in a learned language. Two of the five English mystics are women, a staggering thought considering that neither would have received an education approaching that of their male counterparts. But it does make sense when considering what they were writing about. By using the vernacular, they could couch their theological ruminations more as personal encounters with the divine, rather than present them as treatises on the nature of the divine.

That a woman could have an individual experience and relate this to her relationship with Christ was preferable to trying to take on the monasteries and universities with academic treatises. Mystics directly experienced God in three ways: first, bodily visions, meaning to be aware with one's senses – sight, sound or others; second, ghostly visions, such as spiritual visions and sayings directly imparted to the soul; and lastly, intellectual enlightenment, where their mind came into a new understanding of God.[6] Julian says she has all three, but wants to explore the spiritual sight more fully:

> All this was shown in three ways: that is to say, by bodily sight, and by words formed in my understanding, and by spiritual vision. But I neither can nor know how to disclose the spiritual vision as openly or as fully as I would wish.
>
> (Chapter 9)

Had she tried to do this via the traditional routes reserved for theologians – namely within a university or monastery – she would have been prohibited because she was a woman. But within her cell she could read, ruminate and write, and because she wrote a mystical text in English, she could avoid coming into direct conflict with the male intellectuals of her time.

Julian's *Revelations of Divine Love* is as unique for what it is *not* as for what it *is*. It is classed as a mystical text, since it focuses on a set of individual visions and explores a personal understanding of divine matters. Yet it is unlike other mystical texts of the time in many ways because it speaks to 'all fellow Christians' rather than one reader. Julian's femininity brings a new twist to the themes handled by Hilton, Rolle and the *Cloud*-author, in particular with regard to God's unconditional love as mother. Unlike other fourteenth-century religious texts, Julian's is not founded on scholasticism or theological texts, it is not biblical in focus, and there is no mention of the multitude of biblical characters, from Adam and Eve to the Apostles. It is not instructional, and gives no direct guidance on how Christians should live their lives. It is not like other vernacular literature, such as Chaucer or Langland, in that it has no cast apart from Julian herself, God, Mary and Christ. It is not poetry, yet it is poetic. It is from the fourteenth century, and yet it seems timeless.

It is the work of one remarkable woman who has contemplated a set of personal visions within a single room for decades. The idea of being walled up in one room for the rest of our lives – more than two decades in Julian's case – may sound like a living hell. That men and women throughout the medieval period chose this life chimes with our modern notions of the time as backwards, superstitious and ignorant. However, the life of an anchoress was something middle-aged women like Julian could embrace. If she were a widow or unmarried, there were four options she could choose from: marry again, become a celibate laywoman, enter a convent or become an anchorite. Julian chose the latter.

Julian as anchoress

The word 'anchorite' comes from the Greek verb 'to retire'. An anchorite had to retire from the world, in emulation of the fourth-century Desert Fathers who sought to retreat from the world in order to be less distracted and more focused on spiritual matters. The desire for a hermit's life away from cities and people was countered by the monastic ideals of communal living and adherence to a strict rule. But by the eleventh century a new interest in eremitical removal from worldly concerns became increasingly popular. Some chose the life of a solitary, rather than a hermit, so Richard Rolle, for example, was able to move about and was not tied to one place.[7] In the fourteenth century there were options for those who wanted to follow the example of the original desert hermits. Yet there was a major difference: while the Desert Fathers had left behind the city in search of peace, medieval solitaries, anchorites and their female equivalents, anchoresses, were often walled up in the heart of towns. They were 'in the world, but not of it'.[8]

A text survives from the thirteenth century, called *Ancrene Wisse*, which details the role of an anchoress and what was expected of her: 'True anchoresses are indeed birds of heaven,' says the author, 'which fly up high and sit singing merrily on the green boughs – that is, direct their thoughts upwards at the bliss of heaven.'[9] An anchoress should be seen as a potent member of a medieval society that valued continual prayer and care for the spiritual needs of its citizens. In a reductive version of medieval society – the three estates – the clergy protected the people's souls, the nobility protected the people's rights and the peasantry provided for daily needs. But certainly those members of society actively involved in religion, such as monks, priests and hermits, were fulfilling a function. As an anchorite, Julian would have imbued the very fabric of her church with her prayers and meditations, something the Christians of Norwich would have prized. She was working for her community, fighting for the souls of the people with her prayers.

Yet the *Ancrene Wisse* hints at some of the challenges she would have faced. Her contact with the world was strictly limited to conversation behind a black curtain and restricted interaction with her servant. She would have a window to the world, but it was to be seen as a distraction: 'My dear sisters, love your windows as little as ever you can . . . all the misery that there now is and ever yet was and ever shall be – it all comes of sight.'[10] Julian was in the world, but her text reveals she sought to withdraw from it, into a complex and mentally challenging inner life.

There were many restrictions on Julian as an anchoress. Not only had she to adhere to the three regulations of poverty, chastity and stability of place, she could also not converse with men, unless it was observed, and she was to restrain herself from becoming involved in teaching young girls or protecting valuables. In a turbulent time, the relative security of an anchor-hold (an anchorite's cell) would have made it a logical place to keep wealth and possessions safe from plunderers or rioters, but guides for anchoresses stress that this is strictly prohibited. And as far as teaching goes, the wisdom of a wise woman may well have been attractive to young girls, seeking a mentor to educate them. Julian may have taught a little, but she was supposed to live apart from the world, so could not do so actively. She could, however, keep a cat to deal with mice and rats. So was born a popular image of Mother Julian with her cat curled up by her feet as she wrote *Revelations of Divine Love.*

Being withdrawn from daily life – its distractions, noise, responsibility and problems – allowed her to immerse herself in rumination and meditation, seek deeper spiritual understanding and even write down her ideas for posterity. In the fourteenth century, most women's roles were clearly defined and largely revolved around caring for the household. As wife or mother, a woman would have had a constant cycle of chores to complete, from preparing food and fetching water to looking after her husband and children. As a nun, she would have had an equally full schedule, her monastic responsibilities arranged around the strict religious hours. Whether she had chosen the life of wife or nun, Julian would have had a busy life, with little spare time to sit quietly, ruminate on her visions, and write.

Julian declared she had her revelation many years before she entered the anchoress cell. A number of years passed between experiencing her visions and taking the decision to cut herself off from the world in order to understand them more fully. Perhaps it took the death of a husband or children for her to let go of her worldly responsibilities and become an anchoress. Whatever the trigger, the opportunity for individual study and betterment, silence and rumination would have seemed an attractive proposition to Julian. Her life inside the cell would have been ordered, but not in the rigid way a nun would experience. She would probably have kept monastic hours, with prayers set at seven times daily. The clock at Norwich cathedral had chimed the time since the start of the fourteenth century, so Julian could keep track of her hours by listening for it. Yet she was free of the many other responsibilities imposed on nuns, such as tending to the livestock, embroidering and cleaning. She largely managed her own time, was safe within her anchor-hold, and had the freedom to think, read and write.

Yet the life of an anchoress was not to be entered into lightly. The rites of enclosure that Julian would have undergone when she entered her cell are variously reported, but all include the implication that the woman is dead to the world. She would be led to her anchor-hold as a requiem Mass was sung, would then receive extreme unction, reserved for those who are about to die, and would have had dust sprinkled over her to symbolize that she was being buried: 'ashes to ashes, dust to dust'. The door to the cell was then bolted from the outside, with wax seals applied, or in more extreme cases, a brick wall built to seal it up permanently. An anchoress was then not allowed to leave her cell again on pain of excommunication.

It was an extreme, dramatic, perhaps even disturbing ceremony to sit through, for both the congregation and the anchoress. The bishop would possibly have presided, as it was an important religious commitment that required sanctioning by the highest members of the Church. To see a living person given the rites of the dead, then led away never to be seen again must have been intensely moving for all involved. The fact that Julian chose enclosure for the rest of her life indicates she must have been a devout, serious and focused woman. But so many other questions remain. Who was she, why did she choose to be enclosed in her forties, why did she want to write, and what life had she had before she dedicated herself to writing *Revelations of Divine Love*?

The real Julian

Many have speculated on the woman behind the name, 'Julian of Norwich'. It has been difficult to access the real identity of the author of *Revelations of Divine Love*, despite stoic research. Some scholars argue that she must have been a nun who entered an anchorite's life after many years within a convent, possibly the famous Carrow Abbey in Norwich. Others argue that she was probably a laywoman, perhaps with a husband and children whom she lost to various plagues. Others still feel they can identify her with a specific local noble family, and pinpoint the place where she grew up. All we can know with certainty comes from Julian herself in small details she scatters through her book, although she gives very few clues.

A recent work on Julian seeks to identify her with one documented woman, Julian of Erpingham.[11] She grew up as a member of one of the foremost noble families in Norwich, and her childhood home was 60 King Street, just a stone's throw from the Church of St Julian and the anchorite's cell. The architect responsible for rebuilding Julian's cell in the 1950s, after the site was severely damaged in the Second World War, researched all women with the name 'Julian' mentioned in fourteenth-century documents around Norwich. One name is prominent but disappears suddenly, with no record of death, at the time that Julian of Norwich may have entered her cell – Julian of Erpingham.

She was the sister of a famous knight, Sir Thomas Erpingham, who fought at Agincourt and had been a trusted friend of King Edward III. Julian, his elder sister, is recorded as marrying twice, her first husband dying in 1373 – the same year as our Julian records receiving her revelations. Could the death of her husband have instigated a life-threatening sickness? The dates certainly match up. Julian of Erpingham remarries following her first husband's death, and has three children. This fits with the homely and motherly tone of *Revelations of Divine Love*, which abounds in descriptions and details that an enclosed nun would not necessarily focus on so heavily. Indeed, despite suggestions that Julian of Norwich had been a nun at nearby Carrow Abbey, it is almost certain she had not spent her early life within a convent. There are no references whatsoever to the monastic way of life, and instead the book abounds in incidental descriptions of domestic settings, and the life of a wife and mother.

By 1393 Julian of Erpingham's second husband had died, her eldest daughter had married and her youngest was possibly fostered out – this is the date by which many believe the author of *Revelations* entered her cell. With two husbands dead, three children out in the world, and a set of revelations to ruminate on, the choice of enclosure as an anchorite at this stage in life may have seemed attractive to Julian of Erpingham. The legacies from two husbands would have meant she had the means to support herself. For an anchorite to be looked after by a maid, and provided with food and comfort for decades, was a costly affair. Any bishop interring an anchorite would want assurance that her family would be able to cover the costs.

It is impossible to state with certainty that Julian of Norwich was Julian of Erpingham. True, the male name is relatively rare in the late fourteenth century, and the dates of revelations and enclosure seem to fit. But *Revelations of Divine Love* remains as potent and significant whether we connect the author with an identifiable individual or not. Unless more documents come to light directly connecting Julian of Norwich with a historically verifiable individual, she will have to remain largely unknown. All we can know for sure is what she tells us in her book, and at the heart of that lie sixteen revelations received on 8 May 1373. This is the one date in Julian's life we can be certain of, and it plunges her into the heart of one of England's most turbulent periods.

2

Julian's life and times

Julian in Norwich

Medieval Norwich was a vibrant, exciting and cosmopolitan place. Through much of its history it was England's second city, and it still has more medieval churches than any other city north of the Alps. In Julian's lifetime it was at the heart of the primary mercantile area in the country, and covered an area larger than London. It was dominated by the castle (built around 1100 under the Normans) and the cathedral (which was finished around 1145). Norwich became important in terms of trade due to the rich supply of wool gathered from the Norfolk sheepwalks.[1] It had a warehouse for the Hanseatic League (the countries crossing from the Baltic to the North Sea), and goods crossed freely from the River Wensum to Northern Europe.

Its streets were peppered with guilds, monasteries and friaries, so ideas, money and information could change hands freely. The major ecclesiastical buildings in the city were the cathedral and its attached Benedictine Priory, which boasted one of the richest libraries in the country. Yet there were also representatives from the diverse spectrum of fourteenth-century religious groups in Norwich, from Dominicans to Franciscans, with evidence for some less common orders, such as the Beguines. These were semi-monastic laywomen, who emulated the example of Christ by caring for the sick, embracing poverty and devoting themselves to prayer. They were closely associated with the cloth industry of the Low Countries, so their presence in Norwich during Julian's lifetime was no doubt a result of close trade links between the city and Flanders. Although they were outside the traditional monastic orders, the Beguines may have influenced Julian's spirituality, given their origins as laywomen who rejected their traditional roles in favour of devoting themselves to following Christ's example. Julian certainly implies she was aware of the Beguines' focus on caring for the sick in her *Revelations*, but this could also simply be something she was exposed to while living in the world and tending to friends and family afflicted by illness.

We can position Julian firmly within the busy streets of Norwich. There are a number of references to 'Julian the anchorite, living next to Saint Julian's Church in Norwich', so we have historical evidence to work from. One Richard Reed bequeathed two shillings to 'Julian anchorite', while Thomas Emund, in 1404, leaves twelve pence to Julian and eight pence to Sara, who was 'living with her'.[2] This was probably her maid, who would have had access to her via a smaller cell attached to Julian's. She would tend to the anchoress's physical needs, providing her with food, drink and clothing, cleaning the cell and removing any waste. She may also have brought Julian books and writing material, and arranged visitors to her cell. Her maid was her link with the outside world, and Sara no doubt also brought news and gossip to Julian.

It is important to remember where Julian's cell was located. It was on the main thoroughfare through Norwich, close to the docks and also the 'red-light district'. Her curtained window offered people the opportunity to speak with her, confide in her and learn from her. In some ways Julian's role as anchorite crossed over with that of social worker or agony aunt, in that she provided advice and support for those who sought her out. Julian would have encountered all manner of people, from poverty-stricken prostitutes to nobility. In the face of this varied spectrum of humanity, Julian does not seem to have been judgemental. Instead she declares in the text that there is no evil, no sin, no judge other than God. There is goodness and love in everyone.

Julian's age (she lived a long life for the time), experience and mystical revelations made her someone to be sought out for both practical and spiritual advice. Many would have visited her cell in order to speak with her through the black curtain of her window, which faced on to the street. One such visitor was another female writer of the time, who, fortunately for us, kept a record of her experience.

Julian and Margery

Some time around 1413, shortly before her death when she would have been over seventy, Julian was visited by Margery Kempe, a noblewoman from nearby King's Lynn. Margery attests to this in her own work, *The Book of Margery Kempe*, which is another remarkable survival from this time and place: the earliest surviving autobiography in English. 'And then she [Margery] was commanded by our Lord to go to an anchoress in the same city who was called Dame Julian.'[3] There was a thirty-year age difference between the two women, and Margery was no doubt seeking the wise counsel of an older visionary to find validation of her own experiences.

Following the birth of the first of fourteen children, Margery Kempe had been afflicted with suicidal thoughts and uncontrollable tears, which made her a difficult character for the established Church to contain. After the birth of her last child, she managed to convince her husband to agree to a celibate marriage, and instead imagined herself married to Christ. On the one hand, her copious crying, tendency to collapse in public places, and visions were all possibly mystical experiences. However, unlike Julian, Margery was very public about her mysticism; and her many travels, both around the country and across Christendom on pilgrimage, made her a more obvious problem. Margery visited Julian at a point in her life when she had already been on the receiving end of harsh criticism for her visions, and she was no doubt seeking support from a fellow female mystic.

As is characteristic of Margery, her main focus in her conversations with Julian was herself. She presents the anchorite with tales of her experiences, her 'compunction, contrition, sweetness and devotion, compassion with holy meditation and high contemplation, and full many holy speeches and conversations that our Lord had spoken to her soul, and many wonderful revelations.' Margery dictated her life to a scribe, who seems to have captured the dialogue between the two women in a remarkable way. Julian's voice comes through in her response to Margery. She is positive and delighted by the visions, but cautions Margery with her characteristic balance and restraint: 'As long as it was not contrary to the worship of God and the benefit of her fellow-Christians; for, if it was, then it was not the inspiration of a good spirit but of an evil spirit'.

As in Julian's *Revelations of Divine Love*, Margery's book reports Julian's reference to the recipient of visions as a simple 'creature'. The themes that preoccupy the anchoress recur in *The Book of Margery Kempe*, with a focus on sin and forgiveness, a rejection of earthly concerns and a focus on the love of God. Margery emphasizes her own concerns, of course, stating that Julian encouraged her with 'weeping so plenteously that the tears may not be counted', and stressing that the scorn she receives is an indication of her merit. This single passage reveals a good deal about both women, and also indicates how receptive the medieval female memory could be to orated speech and instruction.

Given the mystical nature of her visions, her openly unconventional behaviour and her habit of preaching on her travels, Margery was in danger of being burnt as a heretic. She is another female writer whose work was nearly lost, but again we are fortunate to have such a fascinating surviving document of a medieval laywoman's life and times. Her account adds flesh to Julian's in terms of historical and social context. She grew up in Kings Lynn, which was an important Norfolk port like Norwich. She was from a grand noble family, and married John Kempe, who was from a prosperous mercantile family. Unlike Julian, however, Margery's account is firmly rooted in her earthly life. The reader learns how her visions were prompted by a severe illness (possibly post-natal depression) suffered after the birth of a child. Her account brings medieval Norfolk to life, with its colourful characters and important locations at the heart of her narrative.

She has a very different approach from Julian in terms of her writing style as well. While Julian's text is full of desire, Margery displays a deeper obsession with passion and sexuality. She states she wants to be punished for a 'sin' she wished to confess, which may have been adultery, and there is a continuing obsession with forgiveness throughout the text. In describing her visions she illustrates a sexually fuelled relationship between her and Christ. They have a conversation after which he 'ravishes her soul'. Naturally, she was worried her visions could be coming either from God or from the devil, and this is something she discusses with Julian. This was a problem underlying medieval women's visions; they are unable to discern their origins, and to determine whether they are from good or evil sources. It was in a vision that Christ told her to see Julian, and the reassurance of this wise, elderly visionary must have been a great comfort to the worldly, vocal, socially engaged Margery.

Julian was known for her exemplary life rather than her visions, which she most probably kept secret during her time in her cell. She did not 'trade' on them, like Margery, who was paid to pray for people, was welcomed to dine in great houses wherever she travelled, and treated like a celebrity. This notoriety was not easy for Margery at times. She travelled widely on pilgrimage, without her husband, and was abused and vilified by fellow travellers. More seriously, she was bordering on heresy by publically preaching her visions and ideas. She had a particularly difficult encounter with the Bishop of Lincoln, who tried to question her for Lollardy (see pp. 27–9) because she travelled about and preached.

The persecution that Margery experienced may provide another dimension on the anchoritic life Julian chose. Within her cell she was largely protected from accusations of preaching and heresy, she did not have to be judged by those she encountered and she could record her visions for herself, rather than relying on scribes as Margery did. Of the two writers, Margery has aged worse. Her love of pilgrimage, indulgences and her vociferous mysticism has meant that her book seems firmly rooted in the religion, society and politics of fourteenth-century Norwich. Margery has not been made a saint, despite the reputation she crafted during her lifetime. She was very much of her world, while Julian seems to transcend it. There is an almost remarkable absence of historical references in *Revelations of Divine Love*. Julian lived through turbulent times, but her work moves beyond the politics and issues that surrounded her, in search of more eternal truths.

The Black Death and fourteenth-century politics

It is possible to read Julian of Norwich's *Revelations of Divine Love* without understanding the times in which she wrote. The image of her that is repeated in stained-glass windows and mass-produced icons is of a woman in a wimple, perhaps dressed a nun, often with a cat at her feet, engrossed in reading and contemplation – a lasting vision of a calm life removed from chaos. However, her text becomes all the more remarkable in terms of its optimism and reflection of an all-loving, all-forgiving God when considered against the dramatic backdrop of late fourteenth-century religion, politics and conflict.

Julian lived through the aftermath one of the most extraordinary moments in human history – the Black Death, 1348–9. The effect on the population of England was devastating, with areas of the country unable to recover to pre-plague numbers for many centuries. East Anglia was the county worst hit by the Black Death, because of the constant stream of trading ships, bringing with them infected rats and people. It is estimated that in Norwich 7,000 of the 12,000 inhabitants died.[4] It turned the social spectrum on its head with its lack of concern for class; the three strands of medieval society – nobility, religious and peasantry – were hit equally hard.

The feudal system that had been in place for centuries was unsettled as a depleted peasantry could now demand better pay in the face of a dwindling workforce. Julian sets her *Revelations* firmly within the medieval feudal structure, referring to God as her 'lord', and a society where a 'lord' would not condescend to care for his 'servant'. Yet she includes an interesting reversal of this relationship in her parable of a lord and servant, which frustrates the established situation, with a lord lovingly rewarding his servant. So even in her text the transformation of the status quo is emerging. A social system that had been in place throughout Western Europe was beginning to unravel, and people were finding their lives turned upside down by death and uncertainty.

But the Black Death was not the only plague to afflict the people of Norwich. In 1361 another 23 per cent of an already decimated population was wiped out, and this plague was a form that was particularly virulent among children. It continued to hit the forlorn city four times between 1369 and 1387. Julian would have experienced all of these plagues throughout her life, and it was possibly the cause of the life-threatening illness that instigated her visions. Certainly she was affected by the sight of plague victims, describing in characteristically abstract term the horrendous effects of the illness:

At this time I saw a body lying on the earth, a body which
looked dismal and ugly, without shape and form, as it were
a swollen, heaving mass of stinking mire.   (Chapter 64)

Yet despite the horrors surrounding her, and the fact that
many people she would have known and loved were carried
away by the plague, Julian wrote a book that is singularly
optimistic, hopeful and finds a positive path through suffering. With death carts trundling down King Street, past her
cell, Julian would never have felt far from reminders of the
transience of life and inevitability of death.

The physical suffering brought about through plague,
famine and failed harvests during Julian's lifetime erupted
into political turmoil in the Peasants' Revolt of 1381. The
attempts by a royal official to collect poll taxes in Essex
turned into violence, and rallied by the sermons of John
Ball, angry representatives from all sections of society
headed for London. Led by Wat Tyler, the men of Essex
and Kent descended on London, demanding the removal
of unfair taxes, an end to serfdom and the removal of
corrupt government officials. In the rioting that ensued,
prisons were opened, law books were burned and the
Savoy Palace, home of John of Gaunt, was destroyed. The
Chancellor, Simon Sudbury, was beheaded on Tower Hill,
and the revolt was quelled only by the personal intervention
of young King Richard II, then just fourteen years old.

In Norwich the same issues that led the men of nearby
Kent and Essex to march on London had provoked riots
and chaos throughout Norfolk. Geoffrey Litster led a band
of rebels to Norwich Castle, which they pillaged while Litster
feasted. It took the intervention of Bishop Henry Despenser
to suppress the violence. He travelled to Norwich with an

armed force, and defeated the rebels in the Battle of North Walsham. Despenser led the assault himself, gaining the title of 'The Fighting Bishop'. He then personally oversaw the trial and execution of Litster, who was hung, drawn and quartered. He did restore calm to the city of Norwich, but he did so with an iron fist. This is the very bishop who would have validated Julian's request to enter the anchorhold. Despite the fact that Julian herself does not comment on the political and social upheaval of her time, she would have been close to the events physically, as the monasteries and convents around the Church of St Julian and all across the city were plundered. She would have heard the rioting around her, and no doubt feared for her own safety.

Political upheaval close to home was mirrored abroad. The Hundred Years War with France, which raged from 1337 to 1453, had wide-reaching effects on England. French raids on southern English coastal towns were destructive, the military elite was occupied abroad, and trade was affected by difficult relations across the Channel. In terms of trade, Norwich fared relatively well, since the River Wensum provided a safe port on the Eastern coast, which meant merchants from Flanders and Northern Europe could still buy English produce and bring continental goods and ideas. However, with much of the male population of Norwich involved in Edward III's campaigns abroad, the city was lacking strong leadership at a time of economic and social unrest.

This was exacerbated by cataclysmic change within the Church. In 1377, just four years after Julian had received her visions, and a decade or so before she would enter her cell as an anchorite, the Great Western Schism began. For some seventy years the papacy had been based in Avignon, as a Frenchman, Pope Clement V, sought to bind it more closely to the Holy Roman Empire. Seven successive French popes reigned in Avignon, and the papacy fell increasingly under the control of the French court. Yet in 1377 the last French pope, Gregory XI, returned the papacy to Rome. He didn't live for long, dying the following year, and the Church was plunged into a new set of conflicts as rival popes took up position in Avignon and Rome. This wasn't simply destructive in terms of the unity and reputation of the Christian Church. The Schism forced nations and individuals to choose between the rival claimants, and Western Europe was subsequently split along new lines of loyalty to one or other pope.

Bishop Henry Despenser himself took to the front line of this conflict, leading an army of men from Norfolk in support of the Roman claimant. They were lured to crusade by the promise of papal indulgences and the hope of grabbing gold on the Continent. This meant the Church in Norwich, already battered by years of plague, was rudderless. The crusades were ultimately fruitless, and the few who survived, including Bishop Despenser, eventually returned to Norwich humiliated and beaten. At its very highest levels the established Church was seen as corrupt, money-grabbing and violent. And as the Church's leadership continued to flounder, it also found itself challenged at grass-roots level by a growing religious movement that would unsettle communities from the inside, leading ultimately to the Protestant Reformation.

Lollardy and printing

At the end of the fourteenth century the established Church was in disarray. A leading Oxford scholar in Julian's time,

John Wycliffe, introduced an alternative set of ideas for disenchanted, disenfranchised Christians. He attacked the luxury of the priesthood, the selling of indulgences, the veneration of the saints and the very existence of the papacy. Alongside this, he also translated the Bible directly from the Vulgate into English; a radical step, which meant people could access the Scriptures themselves, without the intervention of priests. These ideas were to form the basis of the Protestant Reformation some century and a half later, and his followers would become known as Lollards. That Wycliffe's version of the Bible in English gained great popularity is attested to by the large number of surviving copies – over 150 partial or complete versions, despite the fact that it was a dangerous book to own.

The Peasants' Revolt coincided with a climax in Wycliffe's life and ministry. In the following year, 1382, a remarkable synod was called by the Archbishop of Canterbury to rule on Wycliffe's propositions. An earthquake occurred during the synod (hence it becoming known as 'The Earthquake Synod'), and this was interpreted as God trying to purge London of Lollard heresies. Of the twenty-four propositions attributed to Wycliffe, ten were declared heretical, and fourteen erroneous. This meant that Lollards could now be prosecuted and executed as heretics. It was deemed illegal to own a copy of Wycliffe's Bible, while his many treatises began to change hands secretly.

Unlike Julian, Wycliffe wrote frequently and passionately about contemporary events such is the Black Death. With the loss of many clergy to plague, Wycliffe felt that the spiritual guidance of the people was now in the hands of ill-educated and morally corrupt individuals. He had powerful and influential supporters, including the Queen

Mother, Joan of Kent. Wycliffe argued for 'the invisible church of the elect', a universal church with greater inclusion and sense of salvation. His Lollard followers argued that only God could forgive sin, so confession was unnecessary, and that the worship of relics, as well as bread and wine through the act of transubstantiation, was idolatrous.

The threat these ideas posed to the established Church was huge. Lollards were rounded up across the country and burned as heretics, particularly after the *De Haeretico Comburendo* act of 1401. In Norwich the 'Heresy Trials' led to many deaths, and the site of execution, Lollard's Pit, was right by Julian's cell. Documents of the trials survive, and indicate that a number of women in particular were persecuted. Julian's contemporary and fellow Norfolk female writer, Margery Kempe, was accused of Lollardy a number of times; but Margery was no Lollard. She held to pilgrimage, devotion to the saints, the sacredness of the sacraments, and even survived much of her life on indulgence payments. Yet because she travelled around 'preaching', she was in danger of such accusations. Julian managed to avoid this through being an anchoress, and through her continual assertions that she followed 'true doctrine':

> But in all things I believe as Holy Church teaches, for I perceived this whole blessed revelation of our Lord as unified in God's sight, and I never understood anything from it that bewilders me or keeps me from the true teaching of Holy Church. (Short Text, Chapter 6)

Heresy is a thought crime – it goes on inside of people. Julian would have been aware that she might have been under surveillance, particularly as the Bishop of Norwich, Henry Despenser, was one of the most aggressive traditionalists.

Julian is very careful in her work to accord with ortho-dox Catholic teaching of her time. However, her attitudes towards the forgiveness of sin, salvation for all and the relative exclusion of the saints in favour of direct communion with Christ, may indicate that she was aware of Wycliffe's treatises. In common with many Lollards of her time, Julian connected with the human Jesus, seeing associ-ation with the divine as something a 'simple, unlettered creature' could achieve. What's more, by writing in the vernacular – English – Julian could be seen as part of a broader movement towards sharing ideas, not just with a few Latin-speakers, but with many.

The ideas of Wycliffe and his Lollard supporters would have gained greater distribution through another remark-able fourteenth-century development: the invention of the printing press. It is impossible to overestimate the significance of this in terms of widening access to ideas and information. We today are living through a revolution: the digital revolution. Historians in a century or so will look to the invention of the computer, internet and mobile phone, and see the broader cultural and intellectual changes this revolution brought about. We are in the midst of it, so are still to discover the full implications of global com-munication and instant access to information. But we have the benefit of hindsight with regard to the printing press.

While Johannes Gutenberg is credited with the invention of the printing press around 1440, he in fact perfected a form of printed text that was already in circulation in Julian's lifetime. Block printing had become common in Europe for creating patterns on fabric by 1300, and wood-block images and texts began to be distributed widely. They most probably appeared in Norwich in the late fourteenth century through trade with Northern Europe. The rise in printing coincided with the increased availability of paper, and gradually texts moved away from handwritten manuscripts on vellum, towards cheaper and easily reproduced alternatives. So ideas were moving out of the hands of the few, into the hands of the many.

This was a revolution. The seeds had been sown in earlier centuries, as scribes had branched out beyond monastic scriptoriums into secular workshops, producing handwritten texts faster and more efficiently than their religious counterparts. But with printing, ideas and information could move out of centres of religious influence, into the hands of the masses. As the Black Death and Peasants' Revolt were unsettling the social structure of fourteenth-century England, so printing was transforming its intellectual and spiritual structure. While Julian pre-dates Gutenberg's movable type printing press by a decade or so, she would have been aware that intellectual change was sparking technological development. People outside the court, the Church or the universities could start to share ideas, and her little handwritten book of *Revelations* was created during this exciting moment of change.

What is truly remarkable about Julian is her decision to avoid referencing all these enormous social, political and religious events in her work. She navigates a path through *Revelations of Divine Love* that looks beyond the turmoil outside her anchor-hold, and sees a set of universal truths that can provide hope at a time of darkness and despair. It is tempting to see the words Julian offers in her book as a condensed form of the counsel she would provide through her curtained window out on to King Street. But despite death, destruction, riots, war and religious anarchy, Julian maintained a hopeful message. Her book is so unique because of, and in spite of, the wider issues of her time.

Wise women have always had a role to play within communities, and Julian could have provided a welcome well of supportive words and consolation for the residents of Norwich through its many hardships. That she could take this role at a time when heretics were being burned for preaching, teaching and spreading religious ideas suggests that she was brave yet sensible. She shared her ideas, yet never came into conflict with religious authorities. One way she did this was most probably to keep her written text with her within her cell, working on it over the course of many decades, and keeping it secret. For a woman to write at all in this era was dangerous, but to write on religious matters at a time of religious turmoil was potentially deadly. But write Julian did.

Julian's education

In her text Julian describes herself as 'a simple, unlettered being', and it seems that she had not received a broad education in the strict sense of the word. She writes in the vernacular – English – which constitutes a wonderful survival for students of English literature, but a problem for theologians, since Latin was the language of the Church. Nevertheless, such contemporaries as Richard Rolle and the author of *The Cloud of Unknowing* also chose English as the most suitable language for recording mystical revelations. The use of the vernacular in these cases was established as a precedent by writers such as Bridget of Sweden, but it also suggests that one's mother tongue is the language best suited for attempting to express the inexpressible.

Opinions on Julian's education range widely, from her being a master of Latin and even Hebrew, to not being able to read at all. It is likely that she had a very basic education before she entered her cell, and yet her time as an anchorite allowed her to develop her reading and writing skills, alongside her theological knowledge. Listening to the priest through the window of her anchor-hold facing on to the church would have exposed her to the Latin mass, as well as the ideas spoken during sermons from the pulpit. She may have had access to books (although even the wealthiest households may only have had about twenty-five at most), brought to her by visitors, but there is little evidence that she had developed a thorough understanding of Latin, since at the two points she quotes in Latin directly she gets the grammar wrong.

Despite declaring herself 'unlettered' (which may mean she knew no Latin or French), Julian would have been exposed to a range of languages in Norwich. It is important to remember the literacy rates at this point in England. Only about 20 per cent of men would have been able to read and write, while the rates for women would have been much lower. Yet the city of Norwich housed one of the busiest ports in the country, and people came to trade there from the Netherlands, Germany, France and Italy. The marketplace would have been awash with different dialects, and from her cell on the main thoroughfare, Julian would have heard many languages from the people passing by. It is also important to remember that mystics were valued for the unadulterated access they received to the divine. By seeming uneducated and untrained in the nuances of theology, Julian would be adding credence to the innocence and veracity of her visions. She received them as a 'simple creature', not someone trained in a university, monastery or cathedral school, or versed in French or Latin.

She certainly went to great lengths in her text to stress she was no teacher (although this may also be a defence against accusations of preaching that were made against Lollards):

> But God forbid that you should say, or take it, that I am a teacher, for I do not mean that, nor did I ever mean that.
>
> (Short Text, Chapter 6)

When she states that she 'cowde no lettre', this may mean that when she entered the anchor-hold she couldn't read and write. Internal evidence in both the Short and Long Texts of Julian suggest that this was possibly an exaggeration, and she did have at least a basic education by the time she was an adult. Perhaps she gained this at the nearby Carrow Abbey, one of the most famous convents in the country, and the convent responsible for the church in which Julian was enclosed. While she was most probably never a nun there, Carrow did run a boarding school for the sons and daughters of noble families in Norwich, providing an education and board up to around the age of ten. Here she could have learnt to read, perhaps a little French, and would have been exposed to some Latin. However, the many years she spent holed up in her anchorite cell would have provided the opportunity to hone these skills.

However she received the education and ideas that are clearly evinced in *Revelations of Divine Love*, it does seem that the work, its arrangement and its words are her own. While Margery Kempe dictated her book to a scribe, the structure of Julian's work, and the ways in which she weaves her thoughts together across sections, suggest that it is all her own conception. The rhetoric she employs is not of the sophisticated type employed in universities or monasteries, but she develops a unique writing style that is powerful and effective. Her use of repetition, particularly in patterns of three, was perhaps self-taught or derived from sermons she had heard, yet she gives it a potency that many other writers do not master. This adaptation of rhetoric is mirrored in her theology.

Unlike many writers in the fourteenth century, Julian would not have been trained in the liberal arts and would not have scrutinized theological texts, as her male contemporary mystic Richard Rolle did at Oxford University. Nevertheless, while apparently anti-theological at points, steeped instead in experiential understanding of the divine through revelation, Julian's text displays a clear grasp of leading theological arguments.[5] She echoes the ideas of Augustine and Thomas Aquinas, to name but two. While she had probably not read much of their work, these authors were the bedrocks of fourteenth-century spirituality, so faithful attention to the words of the priest through her cell window and discussion with educated visitors may have been sufficient to provide her with a sound theological basis for her text.

The ability to retain and repeat information from memory was much stronger in the medieval period, since fewer people depended on written records as reminders. This is clear from Margery Kempe's recorded account to her scribe of meeting Julian, which captures the anchoress's style and phrases extremely well. Julian may also have had an excellent memory, not just for subject matter but also for nuance. In addition to hearing theological ideas, she may have been lent books from the Augustinian Abbey across the road from her cell, which she would have read thoroughly and digested. But she would not have had access to the same amount of texts, ideas and debates that many of her male contemporaries could boast.

Her own intellect and brilliance did a lot of the hard work. With a set of sixteen vivid and endlessly unfolding revelations to contemplate, and the relative peace and security of an anchorite's cell to contemplate within, Julian took time to develop her ideas in her own unique way. Her lack of formal education may in fact be the reason why her text is so unlike any others written at the time, since she was writing something original, personal and heartfelt. At the core of the text there is calm and steadiness, brought about no doubt by the stability of place she committed to when she took anchoritic vows. Unaffected by doctrinal nuance and the heady rush of academic discourse, hers is a work that operates on a different level. It rises above day-to-day concerns, theological debate and religious nitpicking, creating instead a more cosmic, timeless view of Christian spirituality. One woman's experiences, and one woman's interpretation of them; yet they can still speak across the centuries.

3

Themes in *Revelations of Divine Love*

On 8 May 1373 Julian had the first of sixteen revelations. Today we might imagine these to be a set of hallucinations caused by fever and the onset of life-threatening illness. Our modern tendency to label mental conditions, or seek scientific solutions for events, can explain medieval mystical experiences through medical terms. Yet Julian would not have seen herself as schizophrenic, or feverish, or delusional. In her view Christ was communicating directly with her, and since she was not creating the visions herself, they must be coming directly from God.

Although her revelations may seem strange to a modern reader, Julian was no more extreme in her experiences than many of her contemporaries. In fact her text indicates that in almost every respect she handles her emotions and visions in a balanced, rational and sensible way, seeking to unpick and make sense of them, rather than punishing her body and soul in search of more mystical encounters. Another mystical writer of the time, *The Cloud of Unknowing* author, cautions that these experiences could be sought out through physical punishment, extreme fasting and bodily asceticism, but that 'they will be illusions, attributable to the devil via their own foolishness'.[1]

Guides for anchoresses stress that they should not punish themselves too heavily, and should eat and drink adequate amounts by fourteenth-century standards. Many would have a staple diet of bread, porridge, ale and wine for feast days. Spiritual writers of the time recognized that unsound body could mean unsound mind, so cautioned against extreme asceticism:

> Wear no iron, nor haircloth, nor hedge-hog skins; and do not beat yourself therewith, nor with a scourge or leather thongs, nor leaded.[2]

That Julian lived a life of moderation and was sound of mind were major considerations in terms of allowing her to become an anchoress. Many were not well suited to the life, either succumbing to extreme loneliness and desolation, or withdrawing for antisocial, rather than spiritual reasons. Before Julian entered her anchor-hold, she would have been interviewed by the Bishop – possibly the worldly Henry Despenser himself – to see whether she had the correct temperament to be enclosed for life. A bishop did not want someone overly extreme as an anchoress under his responsibility, so Julian would have had to pass his examinations to ensure she could endure a solitary life within both her cell, and her mind.

Yet bodily suffering and physical pain were central to Julian's mystical experience. She records wanting to receive a life-threatening illness, which would bring her to the brink of death, at which point she would be saved. This happened to her at the age of thirty and a half. Whether she had contracted plague or another illness, she and all around her believed she would die. She was joined in her sick room by her mother and several others. Days into her sickness she became paralysed, finding it difficult even to move her eyes. She received the last rites, and the priest held a crucifix before her:

> He set the cross before my face and said, 'I have brought you the image of your maker and saviour. Look at it and take comfort from it.' (Chapter 3)

From this image of pain and suffering, Julian experienced a set of encounters with Christ and the Virgin, and she would record these as vivid personal scenes that sparked further echoes, associations and connections.

On the back of these visions Julian listed three gifts she wished to receive:

> This person had already asked for three gifts by the grace of God. The first was to relive his Passion in her mind; the second was bodily sickness; the third was that God would give her three wounds ... In this sickness I wanted to have every kind of suffering in body and spirit that I would have if I were to die, with all the turbulent terrors and tumults caused by devils, and every other kind of pain, short of the soul's leaving the body. (Chapter 2)

This may seem like a startling request – to want to reach the very edge of death and have a true experience of dying. Yet it taps into a deeper current in medieval spirituality, which saw identifying with Christ's pain and suffering during the crucifixion as key to creating a stronger bond of love and understanding with him. After the Black Death, attitudes towards death seem to have changed, with more artworks and texts focusing on impending mortality. To reach the point of death, yet make a recovery, was seen as a 'gift from God' by Julian, as it allowed her to live out the rest of her life with an appreciation of his suffering. The illness was a dress rehearsal for death, and although she did not expect to survive, the fact that she did enabled her to dedicate the rest of her life to achieving a fuller understanding of her visions. An experience of death also brought something else to Julian; an ability to cut through the trivia of life, and see to issues of more lasting significance. Today people who have a near-death experience often report how it made them value the important things more, and Julian's seems to have had the same effect.

Contemplating the crucifix

One aspect of Julian's work that can unsettle modern readers is her fixation upon the wounds, blood and bodily suffering of Christ. Near the opening of the *Revelations* she describes with graphic and expressive terms the sight of Christ on the cross:

> After this my sight began to fail, and it all grew dark around me in the room, as dark as though it had been night, except that in the image of the cross there remained a light for all mankind, and I never knew how. Everything other than the cross was ugly to me, as if much crowded with fiends.
>
> (Short Text, Chapter 2)

While some might feel that the sight of Christ hanging on the cross would be a horror, Julian in fact finds it beautiful and comforting, with everything else being 'ugly to me'. But Julian doesn't stop at contemplating the pain of the crucifixion. She scrutinizes the event in microscopic detail, describing the globules of blood that trickled down from the crown of thorns, and the way it pours out 'freshly and plenteously'. At one particularly graphic moment, she contemplates looking through Christ's wounds, inside his body:

> Then with a glad expression our Lord looked into his
> side and gazed, rejoicing; and with his dear gaze he led his
> creature's understanding through the same wound into
> his side within. (Chapter 24)

The fascination with this sort of description is best exemplified in our modern day passion for horror literature and film. We still have a fixation with the violent, bloody and gory aspects of life. Yet in the medieval period this connection with Christ's suffering was encouraged by the Church, as connecting with Jesus through his pain was seen as a means to get closer to a spiritual understanding of him.

Christians would scourge themselves, wear thorned crowns, deprive themselves of nutrition and lacerate their bodies in an attempt to connect with Christ's agonies at the crucifixion. This is reflected in the genre of hagiography, saints' lives, where saints are celebrated for the torture and pain they endured. The more pain the better, as is rather comically reflected by the third-century martyr, St Lawrence. While being roasted on a gridiron by his persecutors, he lightly remarks 'I'm well done. Turn me over'. He has subsequently become patron saint of chefs and cooks.

This obsession with pain is also reflected in the art of the fourteenth century. *Transi* tombs began to appear, where a decomposing and agonized corpse is sculpted to sit below the more idealized image above. While the sculpture above shows the deceased in all the finery of life, including heraldry, weapons and fine clothing, the image below has a skeletal figure, often being eaten by rats, with entrails and flesh visible. The earliest known example of a *transi* memorial is in Brightwell Baldwin, Oxfordshire, and dates to around 1370. Examples of fifteenth-century cadaver tombs survive from across Norfolk, including those of Richard Howard in Aylsham and Richard Porynlond in St Stephen's Church, Norwich. The practice became more widespread during Julian's lifetime, perhaps in reaction to the devastating effects of the Black Death, which made memento mori (remember that you have to die) all the more pertinent.

The increasingly graphic depictions of death, decay and suffering witnessed in tomb sculpture during the late fourteenth and into the fifteenth centuries is echoed in representations of Christ on the cross. The Despenser Retable in Norwich Cathedral, which dates from Julian's lifetime, shows in minute detail the sufferings Christ endured on the Road to Calvary and on the Cross. This was commissioned by Bishop Henry Despenser, and was just part of a now lost array of religious images that would have bedecked the interior of Norwich Cathedral. The many medieval churches of Norwich would have appeared very different from now. Post-Reformation, the majority of English churches were stripped of their many bright and glittering objects, their painted walls whitewashed or left to erode, and clearer, whiter church interiors became the norm. But the churches and cathedrals of Julian's time would have almost been an assault on our modern eyes, with every surface colourful and decorated. Julian would have visited Norwich Cathedral for special feast days, such as Easter, and seen Gothic images of Christ's suffering on the cross, amid an array of equally vivid and graphic depictions of the martyrdom of saints and the promises of salvation.

It is probable that Julian had a crucifix in her cell, similar to the one she gazed upon during her sickness. It would most likely have been the 'three-nail' type, which was introduced around 1200 and shows both Christ's feet pierced through with one nail. This replaced an earlier version, whereby Jesus either stood on a platform or had both feet pierced, and the single nail at the bottom emphasized the physical stress placed on Christ's arms in order to support his elongated body. It could also been seen to echo the triangular shape of a shield, so creating chivalric associations with Christ whereby he is the rightful and noble 'lord'.[3]

Domestic medieval crucifixes are rare survivals, since they were not valuable, so not treasured, and were commonly made of wood. It is likely almost every home would have contained some religious imagery. The block print was becoming popular, as it was a cheaper alternative to hand-painted images and could be displayed on the wall. Although many crucifixes must also have existed, virtually none have survived. The British Museum has the remains of a simple early fifteenth-century figure, known as the Fiddleford Christ, with evidence of polychrome paint. Red paint has been used throughout to show the path of his blood, from crown of thorns, nails and scourging. Its colour has faded significantly over the course of centuries, so it is now difficult to imagine quite how rich and red the blood would have seemed to a medieval viewer.

Julian was clearly profoundly moved by the vision of Christ's blood on the crucifix that she saw, held before her eyes by her curate as she lay dying. Despite the fact that the original event would have been a largely bloodless affair, with Jesus suffocating from the pressure of hanging on the cross, the image of the crown of thorns generates a great amount of blood in her vision. She describes it in vivid terms:

> At this I suddenly saw the red blood tricking down from under the crown of thorns, hot and fresh, plentiful and lifelike, just as though it were the moment in his Passion when the crown of thorns was pressed on to his blessed head, he who was both God and man, the same who suffered for me in this way. (Chapter 4)

The importance of medieval religious imagery in terms of Julian's own experiences is stressed from the very opening of the book. Were it not for the bloody crucifix the priest held before her dying eyes, she may not have experienced her revelations. The image was the gateway to unlocking a lifetime of rumination on Christ and his Passion. The sixteen revelations all stem from this one image of the crucifixion. This is the centre of the spider's web, and imagining Julian, lying on the floor of her room at the doors of death, a crucifix held before her eyes, it becomes the hub of a wheel of ideas that span out from this potent image of suffering, pain, salvation and hope.

In this respect Julian differs from two of her fellow medieval mystics: Walter Hilton and *The Cloud of Unknowing* author. They caution that the mind should not focus on images but should move beyond these:

> When you pray withdraw your heart from all earthly things, for spiritual things are known by the intellect and not by the imagination.[4]

In the way Julian describes seeing Christ on the cross it is clear she is overwhelmed by the physicality of her visions. She describes the blood in three rather domesticated, normal ways, as pellets, as the scales of herrings and as water dripping from eaves. These are all very homely comparisons, which suggest Julian had run a household in her time before becoming an anchorite. The word 'pellet' seems to refer to a measure of flour, which came rolled up in a ball mixed with cereal.[5] The water running down from eaves would most likely have been a continual trickle, flowing between the reeds on thatched roofs. Finally the herring scales create the impression of Julian scaling a fish, bought from the busy harbour in Norwich. All three are unusual but appropriate images to suggest the globules and trickles of Christ's blood, and show how Julian's mind could leap from a divine revelation to another set of visual recollections. As the eaves, herring scales and pellets are real and tangible, so to her was Christ's blood at his crucifixion.

She seems to be surprised herself at how tangible this blood appears. She could have reacted with histrionics, and her visions could have been laden with sexual references, drama and extreme ascetics. Yet rather than being horrified and disturbed by this vivid, bloody image, Julian says that she finds 'homely comfort' in it. 'Soothly it is more joyful to me than if he gave me great gifts . . . the most joy that might be to my sight.' From the horrors of the world, she moves through the pain of Christ's crucifixion, to a point of transcendence whereby there is complete peace and love in this most vivid of images.

Julian and love

In a time of turmoil, war, conflict between families as one fights for one pope and another for an antipope, and accusations of heresy and death are around every corner, Julian's insistence on the importance of love is startling:

> And he who loves in this way is saved, and so I wish to love, and so I do love, and so I am saved.   (Short Text, Chapter 6)

The rhetorical device of 'the rule of three' serves Julian well here, yet the equation of unconditional love with safety was perhaps a difficult one to convince people of at a time of widespread betrayal and violence. But for Julian love emanates from, and is unconditionally supplied by, God. Her visions focus clearly on the cross, Christ's passion and suffering, yet her mantra throughout is 'love was his meaning'. She even opens the book with the phrase 'this is a revelation of love'. The love does not, however, stem from one direction, from the crucifix before her, or from a god who sits in heaven. Her concept of God is not of a being 'on high', to whom we look 'up'. Instead, he is in all directions, in everything, everywhere. Her God is in the very ground, and grounds us all:

> there is a spreading outwards of length, and breadth, and of
> height and of depth without end, and all is one love.
>
> (Chapter 59)

The way everything is permeated with love combines with Julian's insistence on our own 'blindness'. According to her vision of God, he has always been present in every-thing, and has always been imparting unconditional love, but our own blindness has made this difficult to see. That her visions open her to the opportunity to see his love is a message Julian repeats again and again throughout her work. While Julian's contemporary mystics, Richard Rolle, Walter Hilton and the *Cloud* author, all write for a specific recluse, giving them individual guidance on their path to salvation, Julian writes 'for all my fellow Christians'. Her world is not stratified into layers of more and less worthy, more and less sinful. Instead she sees everyone as deserving and in receipt of the same degree of God's love.

Another facet of love that Julian develops at something of tangent to her contemporaries is the idea of mercy. The idea of a judgemental God, sitting enthroned at the end of days, sending souls to heaven or hell, is one that was very familiar to Julian. Sermons delivered from the pulpit at weekly mass would contain constant reminders to the congregation that they will be judged for their actions, and many churches would contain 'doom paintings' or images of the Last Judgement. As the Church encouraged people to look to themselves in fear of justice, so the state imposed rigid sets of rules and regulations. As fourteenth-century society was stratified in terms of class and gender, so it was rigidly organized with regard to the justice system.

In 1389, when Julian was a middle-aged woman, a law was passed in Parliament that limited pardons for violent crimes. This reflects a widespread desire to punish malefactors severely, and the punishments were often designed to invoke terror. Public executions were widespread, and were seen as a legitimate form of punishment, designed to combat wanton and uncontrolled violence. Ears and hands could be cut off, individuals could be racked, burned and pulled apart by beasts, people were hung, drawn and quartered, and flogging was common as one of the least violent forms of justice. In the face of such a rigid judicial system, Julian again surprises her readers with the loving concept of mercy she stresses throughout her *Revelations*. If God is all-loving, he must show mercy to those he loves.

Julian does not see justice as superior to mercy, and this is made very clear in the parable of a lord and servant that she includes in the Long Text. Julian recounts how she saw 'two persons in bodily form, that is to say, a lord and a servant'. There is a great bond between the two, and the lord looks on the servant 'most lovingly and sweetly'. The lord sends the servant out on an errand, and the servant willingly rushes to do his bidding 'because of his love to do his lord's will'. Yet the servant falls in a pit and injures himself gravely and ends up 'waiting in woe' because he cannot turn back to see his lord. The lord does not blame the servant, but rather is full of concern and love for him. He could punish the servant for failing to complete his task, falling from his path and erring, but instead he sees that the servant has come to harm because he has been faithfully and lovingly serving him.

The lord then states:

> what harm and distress he has received in my service for love of me, yes, and because of his good will! Is it not reasonable that I should recompense him for his fright and his dread, his hurt and his injury and all his misery?   (Chapter 51)

Instead of judging his servant, he rewards him. The servant's plain tunic is replaced with a glorious, colourful gown. The idea of 'universalism' – the belief that all humankind will be saved – is strong here, and would have sat uncomfortably alongside traditional fourteenth-century Christianity. Yet Julian is stressing the point that a loving lord will be merciful. In place of the biblical Fall, she has the servant literally fall into a pit – something accidental, unintentional and morally neutral.[6] The love of God means that there is no suggestion of forgiveness in this parable, since that implies rules and judgement. Instead there is pure compassion, as the lord feels the love of his servant and reciprocates this love. Julian is sailing close to the wind here, and the parable of a lord and servant is one point in *Revelations* where Julian shows quite clearly her tolerant stance in contrast to the more judgemental teachings of 'Holy Church'.

Julian's understanding of love is not that it moves in one direction but that it is entirely reciprocal. She receives her visions because she already loves God, and as she contemplates them, withdraws to her anchor-hold and continues to ruminate on Christ's Passion, she grows in love. In turn she receives more understanding that 'love was his meaning', and all pondering on her visions will continue to lead back to that one revelation of love:

> And fifteen years and more later, I was answered in my spiritual understanding, and it was said: 'Do you wish to know your Lord's meaning in this? Be well aware: love was his meaning. Who showed you this? Love. What did he show you? Love. Why did he show it? For love.
>
> (Chapter 86)

This love is unlike that described by other theologians of the time, particularly in one respect; Julian likens it consistently to the unconditional love of a mother.

God as mother

There is an interesting difference between the Short and Long texts of Julian's *Revelations*. In the shorter text, which she may have had recorded earlier in her life, she shows an awareness that her femininity holds her back. In distancing herself from accusations of 'teaching' or 'preaching', she writes:

> for I am a woman, ignorant, weak, and frail. But I know very well that what I am saying I have received through revelation from him who is the supreme teacher.
>
> (Short Text, Chapter 6)

Yet when she reworks her ideas in the Long Text the insecurities in her gender, and also her education, are removed. Instead, the longer version attempts to work the female aspects of spirituality, revelation, and even the divine, into the text more completely.

A theme that has caught the attention of feminist readers of Julian's text is her understanding of God as both loving father *and* mother.[7] Out of 86 chapters, five are dedicated to expanding the idea of God as mother. This sounds radical from a modern perspective: were medieval writers, with their misogynistic treatment of women, really able to conceive of the deity in female terms? Julian was in fact following a tradition of perceiving God as mother established centuries earlier, and expanded by such writers as Bernard of Clairvaux and Anselm of Canterbury. In this respect she is not revolutionary, and is treading on suitably traditional ground.

However, the ways in which she expands this idea, bringing her own femininity into the accounts and creating a homely image of God, are unique and fascinating. What's more, she does not simply introduce the idea of a feminine aspect to God to create emotional impact, as earlier writers do. To her, God is equally male *and* female: 'As truly as God is our father, so truly is God our mother.'

Julian's understanding of God as mother is not restricted to five chapters of the book – it permeates the whole, and seems to be a lynchpin rooting all her ideas about the divine. That Julian may have been a mother herself is suggested by the intimate love she describes God having for his creation, and the emphasis she places on seeing God's love as enclosing like a womb. Again, this may strike modern readers as radical, but womb imagery was expounded by a number of medieval theologians. In terms of the design of monasteries, the central cloister was understood as the womb, a place of enclosure at the very centre of the monastery where monks and nuns found sanctuary.

Julian writes of being enclosed in love, like a child in the womb. Whether this comes from theological texts, or from her own experience of growing a child *in utero*, it becomes a powerful image that continues the idea of God's love being everywhere – upwards, in the ground, in all creation, and even inside us:

> For as the body is clad in cloth, and the flesh in the skin, and the bones in the flesh, and the heart in the chest, so are we, soul and body, clad and enclosed in the goodness of God. (Chapter 6)

Julian identifies with the unconditional love of a mother, which 'will not be broken by our offences'. This lies in contrast with the conditional love of a father, who rewards his child for good behaviour. Walter Hilton understands the love of God as achieved by degrees, like an ascent up a ladder. The more sinless a life you lead, the better works you do, the more you will deserve the father's love. Julian's attitudes towards God as mother tie in with her attitudes towards sin. A mother will forgive anything a child does because of the overwhelming sense of love, born from having grown the child inside of herself. This is the love Julian can see in God.

The idea of a mother watching her child in its falling and blindness is also reflected in the system of mercy Julian has developed. In the parable of a lord and servant, the cloak that the servant receives is blue, symbolizing steadfastness. The blue mantle of the Virgin Mary is something frequently emphasized in medieval art, and is bound up with the idea of the mother as merciful. If the servant 'falls', God as mother will look on with mercy, and reward the servant's climb up from the pit.

Julian develops her idea of both God and Christ as mother more fully in the Long Text than in the Short Text. Alongside this, she subsumes Mary within the son, becoming an aspect of the 'sensualite' or humanity of Christ.[8] For her, Christ is the mother and an intimate part of Mother Church. She is not redefining the Trinity, although her conflation of the Virgin Mary with her son is very developed in her work. She very specifically only uses the masculine pronoun when referring to Christ, so phrases will run: 'Our mother Christ, he gave us . . .'. Yet throughout Julian has managed to feminize Christ by conflating him with his own mother, creating an allegory of Mary as understanding, grace and sensuality, combined with Christ as the caring, loving saviour who would die rather than see those he loves suffer. Mary as mother of Christ feels everything, and is the emotional conduit for Julian, herself enclosed in the feelings and emotions her visions have ignited. So she sees her love for Jesus as reflecting that of his mother, and similarly she sees herself as a 'lover' of Christ.

Julian and desire

The potency of Julian's prose is achieved partly through the glorious Middle English in which she frames her thoughts, but also through the vocabulary of desire that permeates the text. Reading her visions can be an unsettling experience, as Julian manages to capture the intensity of what she witnesses through language that makes the reader yearn and ache along with her. This is not the sexually charged description from Margery Kempe, but it is visceral, vivid and emotive. 'From first to last her spirituality is permeated with longing for God.'[9]

Even before receiving her visions, Julian describes how she has a desire for three 'graces' – three experiences for which she longed. She wished to have a recollection of the Passion, a bodily illness that would bring her to death but not actually kill her, and the 'three wounds' of contrition, compassion and longing with the will of God. That a young woman could desire such painful experiences may seem strange, but medieval affective piety was such that it was thought such sensations could bring an individual towards understanding the pain Christ experienced on the cross, and so gain greater unity with him.

> This person had already asked for three gifts by the grace of God. The first was to relive his Passion in her mind; the second was bodily sickness; the third was that God would give her three wounds . . . In this sickness I wanted to have every kind of suffering in body and spirit that I would have if I were to die, with all the turbulent terrors and tumults caused by devils, and every other kind of pain, short of the soul's leaving the body.   (Chapter 2)

It is also important to remember what Norwich was like in young Julian's lifetime. When many family members and friends were succumbing to the most excruciating and painful death brought about by plague, then the opportunity to find solace in Christ's suffering must have seemed like a hopeful perspective on an otherwise bleak outlook. Julian's prayers were answered, and at the age of thirty she was brought to the gates of death by illness. As she had wished, she was then miraculously saved, did not perish, and so could move on through vivid recollections of the Passion to the 'three wounds'. *Revelations of Divine Love* is her response to many decades of extra life she was granted to ruminate on the recollections, and get closer to the contrition, compassion and longing she desired. The longing in particular would preoccupy her to the end of her days.

Women were encouraged to visualize themselves as wedded to Christ, to long for him and to empathize with his pain as a wife would with that of her husband. The *Ancrene Wisse* used vivid language to suggest that the anchoress should see herself as a bride of Christ. Indeed, it was an anxiety of many fourteenth-century writers that solitude and exclusion from community (monastic or lay) could lead to an overly vivid interior life, powered by sensual and sexual imaginings. Although anchoritism was sanctioned by the Church, there were anxieties about the devotional freedoms that might grow within the confines of an unsupervised private cell. Manuals of instruction were designed to guide the anchoress, in terms of both her inner feelings and outer actions.

Another instructional text for anchoresses, *Holy Maidenhood*, contrasts the life of a married woman with that of a virgin. While a wife must submit to her husband's sexual desire and expect domestic violence, endure the vileness of pregnancy and the pain of childbirth, a virgin has a peaceful and elegant life, which will lead to a privileged place in heaven. Sexual desires are to be purged from the anchoress through regular confession to a holy man or cleric, so that they do not stay within and multiply. There were concerns that anchor-holds might be used as brothels, since they were private and unsupervised, but no reports of such activities have survived, which suggests that, on the whole, anchoresses followed the advice of their guides, and suppressed their sexual desires.

The *Ancrene Wisse* accepts that anchoresses will have yearnings, perhaps even sexual ones, while enclosed in their cell. It harnesses these by channelling the anchoress towards Christ, suggesting she consider him her spouse, for to forbid is also to tempt. The union between anchoress and Christ, however, is not couched in the language of the Fall. Instead it is full of desire, but stripped of sexual terminology.

Julian moves beyond the sexually implicit language of fellow female mystics such as Margery Kempe, preferring instead to see desire as something important and purifying. It is only through fully desiring an intimacy with Christ on a spiritual level that she will gain any understanding of the full intensity of his love for her. Throughout Julian's text she speaks of love coming almost relentlessly *from* God, while the individual has to cure himself or herself of blindness and the wounds of sin in order to truly see it. This is not a love-sick woman pining for her lord but rather a slowly unfolding awareness of love, driven by desire to understand and to get closer. Julian's visions leave her constantly out of reach, aware that there is so much more to understand, and the desire comes through most strongly in her continual striving to get to the next point of experiential revelation. Yet one barrier to desire, longing and love is sin; the recurring yoke of previous misdeeds that weighs heavy on every soul.

Julian and sin

The modern view of medieval Christianity is that it was dogmatic, particularly with regard to sin. Numerous images or sculptures survive depicting the Last Judgement, with the saved securing a place in the comfort of heaven, while the damned – the sinners - languish in hell. The Last Judgement would be painted or sculpted on the west door of many churches, or above the chancel arch, where it separated the clergy from the lay congregation. Known as 'doom paintings', these would often be the last thing people would see as they left the church, reminding them that they should avoid sin as they re-enter the world. In Julian's Norfolk there are surviving doom paintings at Attleborough, West Somerton and Bradfield. She would have seen images of the saved and the damned, and her ever-compassionate mind would have worried away at the problem of sin.

Traditionally in representations of the Last Judgement, Christ sits in the centre, with heaven to his right and hell to his left, St Peter guarding one door and the devil the other. In hell, sinners are shown enduring all manner of torments, depending on which sins they committed in life. In the tympanum at Sainte Foy in Conques, for example, usurers are shown hanging from a bag of coins like Judas, adulterers are hung naked next to their lovers, and liars have their tongues pulled out. The many sins (some more heinous than others) a human being could commit were carefully enumerated. Dante describes these most vividly in his *Divine Comedy*, completed before Julian was born, around 1320. By the time Julian wrote *Revelations of Divine Love*, very clear outlines were in place regarding which sins deserved which punishment, and the concept of purgatory was firmly established as 'God's waiting room'. Through payment of indulgences, the patronage of monastic organizations, and a sequence of prayers, individuals could ensure a quicker transition from purgatory to heaven: money talks, and the threat of purgatory for even those who had not committed terrible sins, alongside that of hell, kept clerics, monks and friars in pocket.

In Julian's youth she would have frequently encountered images, texts and sermons encouraging her to veer away from sin, to receive confession and to remember the fate of her soul at all times. When the average life expectancy was around forty, it is unsurprising that people would want to consider a sinless life on earth in exchange for an eternity in paradise. The ideas of heaven, hell, purgatory and the Last Judgement were not something medieval people chose to believe in or not – there was no alternative, and although some may have questioned their exact natures, they were firmly and tangibly believed in. As this earthly life is real, so was the afterlife. This is an important point to consider when viewing medieval attitudes to sin from our modern perspective. To sin was to secure yourself a place for eternity in the never-ending punishments of hell. If you could maintain thirty, forty, fifty years on earth without breaking the rules, you would get a never-ending paradise.

Given the proliferation of images and sermons on sin, Julian's approach to the subject is surprising. True the tide was turning, and the work of Wycliffe and others sought to do away with purgatory, indulgences and confession in favour of seeing God as the only judge. But 'Holy Church', as Julian describes it, was still clear in its attitudes towards sin. 'We might plausibly see the primary theme of the Long Text as the fruit of her meditation on the problem of evil and its remedy.'[10] Surrounded by evidence of sin, in the acts of bishops, crusaders and clerics, and faced with the consequences of evil behaviour, as the Black Death and Great Schism were perceived, Julian had good cause to ruminate on this issue. Yet the conclusions she draws are remarkably open-minded. Perhaps formed through her early life outside the anchor-hold, or through interaction with a cross-section of society at her cell window, Julian declares that 'there is no sin'.

The idea that God himself created no sin is not a new one. That God left a space, if you like, within humanity for 'free will' led to the Fall of Adam and Eve, and to all consequent evil choices made by humans. This was seen as a theological way around the perceived errors of God's perfect creation, made in his own image. Sin comes from our freedom to choose, but never directly from God. Yet this 'free-will debate' is ultimately profitless, since if God is able to create an existence in which sin exists through free will, why did he not choose to create a better world in which there was no sin? This is just one of the cyclically problematic dialogues medieval theologians engaged with. But Julian, in contrast, has a clear, unflinching and unwavering attitude towards sin.

Julian qualifies her ideas on sin with the statement that 'sin is behovely', which is a term at once both ambiguous and distinctly Julian in its intent.[11] 'Behovely' is almost always translated as 'necessary', but this fails to take on board the nuance Julian intended in the word. Rather we should consider that sin 'fits' against a backdrop in which it is necessary, and which makes sense of it. We could call Julian's views 'cosmic' in terms of their reach, summed up by her hazelnut analogy and born from contemplation on the great questions: 'Who am I? Do I exist? What is existence? Do I matter?' A number of 'prayer nuts' survive from the late medieval period. These are often incredibly highly carved, and an example from the British Museum measures 6 cms across. They contain a wealth of religious images for an individual to open up and contemplate, seeking an understanding of deeper spiritual truths through a nut held in the palm of the hand. We could project Julian's ideas into our own space-age time, whereby we contemplate all humanity as atoms within an almost unbearably large universe. On this sort of a scale an individual person's sin becomes part of the fabric; it is necessary in the sense that it exists within a web of consequences and events, but it is still so tiny in the eyes of a loving God.

If a person has sinned, in the eyes of the fourteenth-century Church, then there begins a cycle of guilt, confession and reparation. Yet Julian would argue that it is unnecessary, since sin is 'behovely'; that is, the sin has become part of what has been – it was necessary in terms of its fit within the narrative of existence. To consider that her God, who is forgiving and loving like a mother, would punish his creation for eternity due to an individual sin, already part of the fabric of the past, fails to take account of the breadth of his love.

Seen within a medieval Christian world-view, this divine patience witnesses to the sense that wickedness, destruction and sin are all happening continually on our little planet, but that there is an unfolding of time (what biblical scholars sometimes call 'salvation history'), which means these evils become part of a much wider narrative. In Julian's text this gives rise to a characteristic calm, which comes through most strikingly in her treatment of sin. As she believes that 'all shall be well', so must she believe that 'sin is behovely', since it is part of the unfolding story of God's design. Yet she is not passive in the face of sin:

> We must feel a naked hatred for sin, and love the soul as
> God loves it without end. Then we shall hate sin just as God
> hates it, and love the soul as God loves it.   (Chapter 40)

She believes that, while there is terrible suffering and in-
justice, criminality and cruelty, these fly in the face of the
overall scheme God has devised; a scheme that is founded
on love. If we can sin in the knowledge that God loves us
then that is for our own soul to bear.

There is an interesting change between the Short and Long
Texts of Julian's *Revelations* with regard to sin. In the Short
Text she cites a range of sinners who received forgiveness,
including Mary Magdalene, Peter and Paul, Thomas and
King David. Yet in the Long Text these are replaced with one
fascinating example: the now lost story of St John of Beverley.
We know virtually nothing of this saint, as his life has dis-
appeared along with those of many other British saints:

> in his youth and in his tender years he was a beloved servant
> of God, greatly loving and fearing God. And nevertheless
> God allowed him to fall, mercifully protecting him so that
> he did not perish nor forfeit any time; and afterwards God
> raised him to many times more grace.   (Chapter 38)

In the 1990s a Dutch account of 'Jan van Beverley' was dis-
covered, which gives some flesh to John's story. He was the
son of a powerful English earl, who chose to live as a hermit.
The devil visited him in the form of an angel and told him
he must choose one of three sins to avoid damnation: drunkenness, unchastity or murder. He chose drunkenness, since
he thought this the least damaging of the three. While under
the influence of drink he was visited by his sister, whom he
didn't recognize, then raped and murdered; he committed
all three of the devil's sins. Overcome with grief, he decided

to do penance by walking only on all fours, letting his hair grow all over his body, drinking only water and eating grass, until a newborn child will absolve him of his sin. Seven years later this happens; he returns to his sister's grave to find her miraculously alive, and his sins are forgiven.

If Julian knew an account of John of Beverley's life that had some or all of these elements, then her citation of him as a forgiven sinner is all the more astounding. The fact that it is found in a Dutch manuscript may not be so surprising when considering the trade links between Norwich and Flanders. His saint's life is one of the most dramatic examples of sin, combining the 'hairy anchorite' motif with that of the devil's three temptations. John was a native English saint, and it is likely his story was well known, given the lack of information Julian includes from it. Presumably she thought her readers would know of this legendary sinner. By citing someone with whom people would have been familiar, Julian is holding up a strong and relevant example. She is showing how God's ability to absorb all sin is extended to those who strive through 'service and labour' to love him. She states that she herself had sinned, and yet:

> Our Lord in his special grace visits whomever he wishes with such great contrition, and also with compassion and a true longing for God. Then they are suddenly freed from sin and from pain. (Chapter 39)

It is God who is active in this relationship, not the sinner. God delivers compassion and true longing, which heal and reward the sinner. This is a reversal of 'striving for perfection' presented in Rolle's or the *Cloud* author's texts. If anything, it is sin, both Julian's own and that of all her fellow Christians, that brought about the 'gift' of true longing for God's love.

Sin is the vehicle by which one reaches this understanding, so sin is not just absolved, it is part of what it means to be able to truly engage with God. It is 'behovely'. We need to be wounded in order to heal, and so the wounds of sin are the means by which we recognize the need for mercy, compassion, grace and love. The *Ancrene Wisse* touches on this:

> They who love most shall be most blessed, not they who lead the most austere life, for love outweigheth this.
>
> (*Ancrene Wisse*, Chapter 7)

But Julian extends this even further. It is not about austerity, or forgiveness, or perfection. It is about love. The understanding that God wants to give all his loved ones the gift of freedom from sin through love is a radical and almost unique aspect of Julian's spiritual view.

Julian's strength

A characteristic of Julian's writing that is worth stressing, but frequently overlooked, is the idea of inner strength. At a number of points she emphasizes that, while life can be incredibly challenging, full of suffering, pain and punishments, God wants us to know we are strong enough to survive them because of his unconditional love. She uses the phrase 'you shall not be overcome' in an emphatic way, as the culmination of some powerful rhetoric:

> And these words, 'You shall not be overcome', were said very distinctly and very powerfully for assurance and comfort against all the tribulations that may come. He did not say, 'You shall not be perturbed, you shall not be troubled, you shall not be distressed', but he said, 'You shall not be overcome.'
>
> (Chapter 68)

In response to the age-old question of why a loving God would allow his beloved children to suffer, die, experience hardship, Julian gives this response. The world is full of pain and suffering, and all of us will be afflicted. But because of his love, while we experience the suffering, we will be strong enough not to be overcome. Julian has a remarkable view of time, whereby those things that have happened, and have become the past, do not affect the overall positivity and joy to be found in the eternal love of God. This is what she means by saying 'thou shalt not be overcome'. There will be challenges, but the bigger picture, for those who can see it, is one of positivity and hope. Strength, understanding, compassion, patience; these all have their place, but the ultimate thing to hold on to is that 'all shall be well'.

Julian's *Revelations of Divine Love* is not a self-help manual. It will not give readers a guide to spiritual progress or self-improvement. We cannot learn spirituality according to Julian, but rather it is something that happens to us through being wounded and healed. Instead of trying to improve ourselves on the 'Ladder of Perfection' recommended by both medieval writers such as Hilton and more recent authors of self-help guides, Julian encourages us to see how impoverished, wounded and in need of love we are. Only by removing ourselves further will we see the bigger picture and our part in it. We are ultimately saved and joyful, because we are part of God's love. We cannot make ourselves better, more deserving, more austere, in order to secure this love. We simply have to give ourselves up to it, and then we shall 'not be overcome'.

One of Julian's greatest strengths is to see joy and happiness in spite of pain, sin and suffering. Hers is an incredibly happy text, permeated with optimism throughout, and even revelling in laughter. When she describes how, in the fifth revelation, she saw evil incarnate in the devil, and how it was rendered redundant by the Passion of Christ, she describes laughing:

> At the sight of this I laughed heartily, and that made those who were around me to laugh, and their laughter was a pleasure to me. In my thoughts I wished that all my fellow Christians had seen what I saw, and then they would all have laughed with me. (Chapter 13)

Julian is the eternal optimist, someone we can cling to in dark days because somehow she sees a bigger picture behind the daily chaos. She can laugh at something so terrible because she feels loved, secure and safe. We can read her text and find similar comfort.

Existentialist, transcendentalist, perennialist or unique?

Albert Einstein saw great value in the mystical experience, likening it to his moments of awareness and revelation:

> The most profound and sublime experience of which man is capable is the awareness of the mystical. In it lie the seeds of true science.[12]

To many, the real essence of mystical texts comes from the representation of time and space they present. As a result, mystical texts have not only fascinated theologians, literary scholars and artists, but also scientists, mathematicians, astrologers and philosophers. While most people experience time linearly, with past, present and future lined up as a series of memories, experiences and ambitions, the mystic sees a dimension outside this. Julian describes it as seeing the world as a hazelnut that nestles in the palm of her hand, and she, like the majority of mystics, presents this transcendental perspective as one of positivity, hope and joy:

> And in this he also showed a little thing, the size of a hazelnut, lying in the palm of my hand ... In this little thing I saw three properties: the first is that God made it; the second is that God loves it; the third is that God cares for it. But what is that to me? Truly, the maker, the carer, and the lover. For until I am of one substance with him I can never have complete rest nor true happiness; that is to say, until I am so joined to him that there is no created thing between my God and me. (Chapter 5)

Reaching this level of understanding requires the mystic to leave behind the noise and confusion of daily life, step away to a place of quiet contemplation, and meditate on spiritual rather than earthly matters.

In Julian's 'hazelnut' there is a sense of the fragility of the universe, such a little thing poised on extinction, but there is ultimately hope because it is loved by God. The Canadian astronaut Chris Hadfield took God out of the equation, but what he described of his experience in space had something of Julian's hazelnut about it. Seeing Earth from afar allowed him to perceive in its wars, violence and destruction a longer narrative, by which it will wait patiently across time and stay secure:

> What started seeping into me on, I don't know, my second-thousandth time around the world, seeing all the ancient scars, was the incredible temporal patience of the world.[13]

Julian's quiet calm and patience in her book is in sharp contrast to her fellow medieval mystics, Richard Rolle, Walter Hilton and *The Cloud of Unknowing* author. In their search to achieve perfection, and so deserve the love of God the father, they urge their readers constantly, and at times frantically, to strive in their efforts. 'Quickly, set yourself to work', encourages the *Cloud* author, while Hilton states, 'you must constantly desire and strive'.[14] Julian does not have such an emphasis on the climb of a wretched soul towards perfection. Instead she sees everyone in a child-like state, and uses passive constructions, such as 'we are brought' to suggest a gradual and slow unfolding. This calm tone permeates the text and is perhaps born out of the many years Julian had to slowly analyse and appreciate her own revelations.

The inward gaze of Julian's text could be likened to the work of existentialist philosophers, who look to the thinking and feeling human individual as the gateway to understanding complex truths about existence. Philosophers such as Søren Kierkegaard, who is widely recognized as the originator of existentialism, believed that authenticity was the most powerful way of finding meaning in life. Only by living passionately and sincerely can an individual come to make sense of what appears at times an absurd world. Julian's *Revelations of Divine Love* pre-dates the emergence of existentialism by some five centuries, yet she does present a view that is truly authentic, in terms of being rooted firmly in her own visions and experiences, and that looks beyond the chaos around her to more profound truths. But Julian is no existentialist. The principle of 'existence before essence' would sit uncomfortably with a fourteenth-century Catholic who believed in an all-knowing God who has a pattern in place for his creation. While she does seem to be open to alternatives with regard to predestination, Julian would not have believed so completely in the power of the self to define, craft and create itself.

Julian is no existentialist, although her work could be misread to fit its ends. She can also be read in the light of another important nineteenth-century philosophic movement – transcendentalism. Born of German and English Romanticism, transcendentalists saw the truly self-reliant and resilient individual as the core of community. Certainly, it is the 'littleness' of things that interests Julian, as she seeks to rise above creation to see a broader picture:

> It seemed to me that this little thing that is made might have disintegrated into nothing because of its smallness. We need to know about this so as to delight in setting at nought everything that is made in order to love and possess God who is unmade. (Chapter 5)

Given the transcendentalist's belief that society, its institutions, politics and religion are corrupt, we could see Julian's deliberate silence on the events that surrounded her as a way of tapping into the 'over-soul' of God. The idea of accessing the inner essence of humanity lay at the heart of the American transcendental movement. Yet Edgar Allan Poe claimed it was 'mysticism for mysticism's sake'; something that cannot be laid at Julian's door.

Julian creates an impression of God as the essential essence that imbues, underpins and inspires everything. This universal spirit is something many modern philosophers and thinkers have grappled with. In the fourteenth century, to express an idea of God not as a bearded, judgemental man in the sky but as an essential quality of all creation could be seen as radical. Today the notion of perennialism has been introduced, to express the underlying unifying factors between all world religions and belief systems. This suggests that specific religions are adapted to the social and intellectual needs of a specific place in a specific time, but that individual mystics and philosophers have been able to access a core set of truths. These include *summum bonum*, a belief in an ultimate goodness, which sees individuals as able to achieve communion with God, and an experiential union with the divine. Julian arguably achieved both. While she was *firmly* rooted in fourteenth-century Catholicism, and did not want to be perceived as anything other than a devout follower of 'Holy Church', she was able to tap into these perennial truths as only a few great philosophers have managed.

She can barely see a divide between our own souls and that of the divine:

> God is nearer to us than our own soul; for he is the foundation on which our soul stands . . . for our soul sits in God in true rest, and our soul stands in God in sure strength, and our soul is naturally rooted in God in endless love. And therefore if we want to have knowledge of our soul, and communion and discourse with it, we must seek for it in our Lord God, in whom it is enclosed.   (Chapter 56)

Now we can label this sort of cosmic awareness transcendentalism, existentialism or perennialism. Yet what Julian was doing was something thinkers across time and space have sought to do. Aldous Huxley, the English novelist who wrote *Brave New World*, set in a dystopian London, also wrote a book entitled *The Perennial Philosophy*. In it he drew together the words and ideas of mystics across time, in search of the themes and ideas that united them:

> The rudiments of the Perennial Philosophy may be found among the traditionary lore of primitive peoples in every region of the world, and in its fully developed forms it has a place in every one of the higher religions. A version of this Highest Common Factor in all preceding and subsequent theologies was first committed to writing more than twenty-five centuries ago.[15]

Julian is not a perennial philosopher; indeed, she may have baulked at the way her text has been misread and given New Age slants of every variety. But she was tapping into a mystical tradition that sought access to what Huxley calls 'the Highest Common Factor', and she calls 'the unconditional love of mother Jesus'. Julian was not trying to be a philosopher, but rather was trying to make sense of her own existence and her own visions. That she did so in such a humble, accessible and honest way is perhaps why she is attracting a new readership today. That her message still resonates is testament to the universality of her message.

Despite apparent similarities between these more recent philosophical stances and Julian's *Revelations*, she is not representative of these modern approaches to the divine. Her God, while complex, embracing the role of mother and father, and loving unconditionally, is still a firmly Christian one. Her world-view is framed by the intellectual and spiritual fabric of fourteenth-century Western Christianity, and to use her as a conduit for modern philosophical thought is to do her a disservice. She was not fully of her time, she is not fully of ours; her words resonate across the centuries to all people, but do not need harnessing to a particular group or approach.

Part 2

THE LEGACY

4

A brief history of
Revelations of Divine Love

This is Julian's time. Her words are travelling around the world in the blink of an eye (or the click of a mouse) as interested people from every corner of the globe and every walk of life find solace in her fourteenth-century phrases. For nearly six centuries she had been sidelined, ignored and even vilified by the traditional, all-powerful, male-dominated Church. As male scribes in male universities or monasteries copied the works of the Church Fathers, transforming their medieval collections of religious texts via Protestant and Enlightenment literature, Julian's text all but disappeared. But times have changed, and now the words of an intellectually and spiritually sophisticated woman, writing in English about her personal visions, can find a forum.

Fortunately for both us and Julian, her text has found a way through the centuries – surviving civil wars, bloody revolutions and the deliberate destruction of Catholic texts. It remained in just a handful of later manuscripts, until finally in the twentieth century when her work was copied, printed and disseminated to a wider audience. But how did her text survive when it was precisely the sort of Catholic mysticism that was targeted by centuries of Protestants, denounced as witchcraft by many? Somehow the text left Julian's cell. This sounds like a basic point, but it is worth considering. While *Revelations of Divine Love* was not a clearly heretical text, some of its main themes sailed close to the wind. Julian's insistence on mercy and an all-loving God who recognizes no sin could be seen as universalism, while her theology is not founded on years of scholarship but rather the ruminations of a 'simple creature'. With the burning of heretics taking place virtually outside her cell, she would have been acutely conscious of the need to keep her ideas quietly to herself.

That she wrote them down at all may seem surprising. This was a time of suspicion, when communities were encouraged to look inwards and weed out the stain of heresy. She not only wrote her ideas down once, in the Short Text, but then appears to have returned to her work time and again over the course of many years, refining her thoughts and continually ruminating on her visions. Julian would not have seen her writing as an act of pride or self-aggrandizement. Instead, she seems to be leaving room in her text for others to take it further, and perhaps experience that seventeenth vision that might make sense of hers finally. She produced an unfinished work, where she knew there was more she could explore and expound. But she left the final revelation, number seventeen, to her readers.

It seems unlikely that Julian would have allowed her text out of her cell during her lifetime. Nothing in her *Revelations* suggests she was eager for recognition, so we must speculate on how it reached a wider audience. One possibility is that she gave a copy to a visitor to her cell, perhaps even Margery Kempe, who would have been a sympathetic recipient and would have influential friends in Norfolk who could copy and distribute it. In a time of religious confusion, handling mystical texts would have been a dangerous exercise, especially if they were not verified by a male priest or theologian. Whoever handled Julian's manuscript, he or she managed to take it somewhere safe (possibly Carrow Abbey), where it was copied and preserved. Julian's own reputation lived on long after her death, with new anchoresses taking her name and inhabiting her cell. She was clearly well respected during her life, so there is a likelihood that her text was also treated with respect after her death.

But the climate changed radically as the Protestant Reformation approached. In 1534, just a century after Julian's death, Henry VIII and Thomas Cromwell passed the Act of Supremacy, which redesigned the English Church and fractured it from Roman Catholic Europe. Books were attacked alongside images and religious buildings, leaving a deep scar on the nation's cultural heritage. The dissolution of the monasteries, far from a chaotic riotous attack on these establishments, was largely thought out and planned. Buildings were deconstructed carefully, and stone reused to fashion new stately homes. The collections of great establishments like Glastonbury, Walsingham and the Benedictine Library in Norwich were plundered for 'useful' texts, which would make their way into private collections, while anything seen as potentially heretical would be burned. Catholicism was by no means wiped out overnight, and many devout families created strongholds to protect relics, artworks and books. Certain families, such as the Earls of Arundel, managed to maintain their Catholic status throughout, despite the efforts of Protestant rulers like Edward VI and Elizabeth I. However, the preservation of mystical texts was potentially very dangerous, and those who owned a copy of Julian's *Revelations* could easily have found themselves the subject of a heresy trial.

As Catholic families had priest holes and secret masses, so they preserved texts such as Julian's *Revelations of Divine Love*. It may be thanks to the family of Thomas More, famous Catholic martyr and advisor to Henry VIII, that the text survives at all. His great-great-granddaughter, Gertrude More, was one of nine young, brave, adventurous women (she was 17 and the oldest in the group was 23) who established a Benedictine order of nuns, which has since become based at Stanbrook Abbey in Yorkshire. Along with the chosen abbess, Catherine Gascoigne, these young English girls chose to flee the oppression of Catholics in England, and founded a house in Cambrai, France. Gertrude was not an easy character, and she had many moments when she doubted what she and her fellow nuns were doing. She died very young, at just 27 years old, of smallpox, but her community lived on. The community was one of resistance and intellectual freedom, and in Cambrai it grew while it remained hidden from view.

What is interesting about Gertrude More and her fellow nuns is that when they went to France they clearly took a copy of Julian's *Revelations of Divine Love* with them. It is impossible to know how they got this, but we can speculate that it was passed from hand to hand by Catholic sympathizers, finding itself eventually in those of Thomas More's descendant. The nine young women who founded the order at Cambrai were in search of intellectual freedom; indeed, it was said that Gertrude was such a beauty that she would be married off as soon as she came of age. In an act she saw as divine intervention, she was struck with a hideous disease that disfigured her face, so no man wanted to marry her. But we should see these women as early intellectual pioneers. Restricted by a male-dominated establishment, their adventure to France would see them managing property, educating new English nuns and protecting, copying and distributing texts that resonated with them on a deep spiritual level. For a young woman hoping to study, read, engage with a sisterhood of like-minded women, the opportunity open to the Cambrai nuns was clear. And Julian's text accompanied them on their travels.

A note on the manuscripts

We no longer have the original manuscript Julian wrote, or even a copy that is roughly contemporary. Three complete copies of the Long Text of Julian's *Revelations of Divine Love* survive. Two are in the British Library, and one is in Paris, a reminder that Julian's text travelled with English nuns to France. The two that form the basis of most modern translations are MS Sloane 2499 (S1), and Paris, Bibliothèque Nationale, Fonds Anglais No. 40 (P). There is another early complete manuscript, MS Sloane 3705 (S2), but this is a late seventeenth- or early eighteenth-century modernization and, although more beautifully copied, is not as accurate for translation.

Of the two most reliable copies of the Long Text, the Paris manuscript, is by far the more elegantly written and the easiest to decipher. It contains some passages not found in S1, in particular a revealing account of the soul that contains scatological imagery, describing the necessity of excretion.[1] However, the Paris manuscript displays a greater amount of editorial tinkering, in that certain words are modernized and problematic passages are 'tidied up' and brought into line with more orthodox seventeenth-century approaches. MS Sloane 2499 is perhaps the closer to Julian's original text, inasmuch as it is clearly written in an East Anglian dialect. It is copied in a rather rushed hand, and is difficult to decipher given that the ink has bitten through the paper. It is most likely a copy made by the English Benedictine nuns at their convent in Cambrai, from a now lost medieval manuscript. While it is still up to two hundred years later than Julian's text, it appears to preserve aspects of her dialect and expression that are excised from the Paris manuscript.

MS Sloane 2499 seems most likely to be a close copy of an original or near-contemporary manuscript of Julian's text, one that found itself under the protection of the English nuns in Cambrai. The Cambrai nuns continued to copy Julian's *Revelations*, producing numerous manuscripts with extracts of her book copied out alongside other mystical texts. The nuns, now based at Stanbrook Abbey in Yorkshire, have recently had a number of handwritten manuscripts returned to them that include parts of *Revelations*, revealing that their sisters in France valued the text deeply and wanted to continue its transmission.

It is clear that the convent at Cambrai was protecting Julian's text, because in 1670 the nun's chaplain, Serenus de Crecy, published the first printed version of the text, based on the nuns' handwritten copies of an earlier manuscript. He tinkers with the text, playing down some of the more controversial elements, and yet his version was still met with contempt by Protestant English readers. The book was vilified, receiving harsh reviews, and people were encouraged not to read the 'poisonous' outpourings of Julian's 'distempered brain'. Crecy had made a step forward, however, and the nuns of Cambrai remained fiercely protective of Julian's text.

The reason the sisters of the English Benedictines in France eventually lost their precious copies of Julian lies in another cataclysmic historic event: the French Revolution. As religious tensions grew in France, the leaders of the Benedictine order demanded that the nuns of Cambrai hand over their books for inspection, to see whether there was any stain of heresy in their library. Remarkably, the nuns refused, claiming they would rather see the dissolution of their convent than hand over their books to their male monastic superiors. They must have known texts like Julian's would have been destroyed, so they entered into a stalemate with the order's superiors, refusing to hand over their books.

But the nuns could not resist the scrutiny of the Revolutionary forces, when finally in 1789 they entered their monastery and collected their holdings. Many think of the French Revolution as an attack on the wealthy members of society and the royal house of France. What few realize is that it also attacked monastic communities and the Church with vehemence and violence. From their small community in Cambrai, the English nuns and guardians of Julian's texts were aware their security was under threat. A catalogue of the nuns' holdings was compiled by revolutionary troops, and it still survives in the Municipal Library at Cambrai. It lists a fascinating, diverse and huge collection of over a thousand handwritten manuscripts, and even more printed books, and illustrates how learned the English nuns in Cambrai had become. There are fifteen printed copies of Julian's *Revelations of Divine Love* mentioned, but sadly it seems that the manuscript originally brought from England by the nuns was not listed by the revolutionaries. Everything else was taken, the nuns were given just fifteen minutes to take the possessions they needed, and they were all imprisoned to await their execution at the guillotine.

The English Benedictine nuns from Cambrai shared a cell with sixteen Carmelite nuns. On 17 July 1794 the Carmelite nuns were led to the guillotine and executed, while the English nuns remained in their cell, awaiting the same fate. Fortunately the pioneer of the executions, Maximilien Robespierre, was killed shortly after the Carmelite nuns, so the English Benedictines never made it to the guillotine. Instead, they took the lay clothes of the dead Carmelite nuns, and escaped to England, where they went on to found the convent at Stanbrook. The Abbey still preserves the clothes of the Carmelite martyrs as a relic. With the English nuns and their convent in Cambrai went all possibility of tracing connections to the original manuscript of Julian's *Revelations*.

Yet all is not lost, and miraculous discoveries continually come to light. Somewhere in a French municipal library, or in the collections of a stately home, there may be documents relating to enigmatic Julian. Perhaps, better still, there may be another manuscript, closer to Julian's own words, that could bring us greater insights into this tantalizingly self-effacing woman. Her original manuscript ended up somewhere, and while the chaos of revolution may have scattered it, there may be an old vellum book hiding in a collection somewhere that can get us even closer to Julian's original words, thoughts and ideas.

Modern translations

Based on Serenus de Crecy's version of the text, in 1877 Henry Collins brought the manuscript to a modern audience, with his printed version. But it was Grace Warrack's 1901 account, with its modernized English and sympathetic treatment of Julian's text, that really made *Revelations of Divine Love* popular. Her text has been reprinted many times, and is an achievement akin to Julian's own considering the circumstances in which it was produced. Out of the suffragette movement, and the increasing intellectual and social liberties women were securing by the turn of the twentieth century, Julian's text could finally emerge.

Grace was brought up in a strict Scottish Presbyterian household, where Catholic mystical texts such as Julian's were precisely the sort of works that were not permitted. It is difficult to know what first drew her to seek out this obscure work, listed in the Sloane Collection under 'Witchcraft: Revelations to one who could not read a letter, 1373'. Why did she attempt translating it from Middle English, a language she displayed no previous knowledge of, into emotional and moving modern English? To translate Julian's East Anglian fourteenth-century dialect well, and to create the sort of potent prose translation that Grace managed, is no mean feat. She must have been exposed to some medieval literature before she embarked on this project, perhaps reading Chaucer at school. She was certainly no medievalist, yet she created a clear and emotive version of Julian's text that really captured the public imagination.

Something prompted Grace to leave Scotland for London (despite a woman's travelling on her own being seen as socially questionable in the nineteenth century), to spend a month living in an unfamiliar city, tirelessly transcribing a rather tatty manuscript and translating a text that would have been attacked by her family. There is the suggestion that she may have experienced a period of grief with the death of a dear nephew, and perhaps she found solace in an earlier printed copy of *Revelations*. Yet she displays great spirit and ingenuity in locating MS Sloane 2499 among the British Library's vast collections, and persuading Methuen to publish her translation. Grace shows how the fortunes of women were changing at the turn of the twentieth century, and what better symbol of this than to produce a printed version of a great fourteenth-century woman's ideas?

Grace's translation was hugely popular, and reprinted many times. Thanks to her, Julian's work has remained in print for over a hundred years, with many new translations, articles and books written about Julian and her text. In an interesting twist, Grace left her handwritten notes to Stanbrook Abbey, the current home of the English Benedictine nuns who probably copied out MS Sloane 2499 in the seventeenth century. Grace was corresponding with the abbess of the convent, and her decision to leave her documents to Stanbrook means that Julian's text has returned in some way to the nuns who kept her memory and text alive. The handwritten notes Grace made from MS Sloane 2499 were recently revealed to her descendant, John Warrack, a musicologist married to a historian. The rediscovery of these notes shows how much detective work there still is to be done on Julian's *Revelations of Divine Love*. It really is a text that keeps on giving.

Conclusion

Why read Julian's *Revelations of Divine Love* today? Hers was a voice nearly lost to time, and 'amplifying subdued voices provides a more complete awareness of medieval history and theology'.[2] But more than simply developing our understanding of Julian's time, this book taps into deeper mystical ideas that have run as a steady current across the millennia. Written at the turn of this millennium, Umberto Eco's work *Baudolino* features a female character called Hypatia, apparently descended from the fourth-century female philosopher, astronomer and mathematician Hypatia of Alexandria. The character describes how a group of female thinkers have developed an understanding of the divine, which she calls 'the unique'. To reach the ultimate point of understanding, she explains what has to be done:

> You have to create an absolute calm around you. You remain alone, remote from everything we have thought, imagined and felt; you find peace and serenity. Then we will no longer experience wrath or desire, sorrow or happiness. We will have moved out of ourselves, wrapped in absolute solitude and profound calm. We will no longer look at things beautiful and good; we will be beyond goodness itself, beyond the chorus of virtues, like someone entering the sanctum of a church and leaving behind the statues of the gods as his vision is no longer of images, but of God himself.[3]

This sounds distinctly similar to what Julian achieves. By being walled up in a single room for over twenty years she found serenity, a peaceful place to achieve 'profound calm' and go 'beyond the chorus of virtues'. It is difficult to capture the magnificence of her work in a short introduction. Julian is unlike any other author I have encountered, and the reason her book is becoming increasingly popular now is that her ideas are finally finding a footing within modern scholarship and Western spirituality. Her time is now, and having waited in the wings for centuries, she is ready to be heard.

Julian of Norwich's *Revelations of Divine Love* can obsess readers, captivate them for a lifetime and offer support and solace during times of difficulty. I've interviewed people who have said that her book offered the only beacon of light through such dark times as the death of a child, dealing with cancer and fighting in wars. And it seems her work rewards more, the more you return to it. Thomas Merton, the twentieth-century Trappist monk and mystic, describes how his relationship with Julian's text developed:

> Julian is without doubt one of the most wonderful of all Christian voices. She gets greater and greater in my eyes as I grow older, and whereas in the old days I used to be crazy about St John of the Cross, I would not exchange him now for Julian if you gave me the world and the Indies and all the Spanish mystics rolled up in one bundle. I think that Julian of Norwich is with Newman the greatest English theologian.[4]

Professor Vincent Gillespie describes it as 'one of the first great masterpieces of English prose . . . in terms of the sheer beauty of her prose there's nobody else at that period who I think can really challenge her',[5] while Rowan Williams states, 'she is blazing a trail, doing something unprecedented'.[6] If Chaucer is the father of English poetry, then Julian is the mother of English prose. But what she produced was something beyond beautiful English literature. She crossed the boundaries between theology, philosophy, psychology, art, science, astrology and even metaphysics. Her relevance as a great fourteenth-century brain is staggering, but her role as a woman in this world of male intellectualism is something that also should be celebrated.

Julian had the ability to do something that very few of us possess: to see beyond our current miseries, the pains and problems that obsess us, the politics that surround us and the events that play out during our lifetimes. Her book is ahistorical, in that it passes beyond earthly things. She is quietly confident that, no matter what seemingly important events are playing out on earth, 'our heavenly mother Jesus cannot allow us that are his children to perish.'

Revelations of Divine Love was written against its own politically, socially and economically unsettled backdrop; every generation struggles to put its own hopes, fears, obsessions and concerns on to a broader canvas. And that is why, like many others, I continually return to Julian's deceptively simple words, which exist outside time and will always ring true whenever and wherever they are read:

All shall be well, all shall be well, and all manner of things shall be well.

Notes

Preface

1 Sheila Upjohn, *All Shall Be Well: Revelations of Divine Love of Julian of Norwich: Daily Readings from The Revelations* (London: Darton, Longman & Todd, 1992), p. x.

2 From the address during the weekly Papal Audience, St Peter's, Vatican, 23 March 2016.

1 Introducing Julian

1 Frederick Christian Bauerschmidt, *Julian of Norwich and the Mystical Body Politic of Christ* (Notre Dame, IN: University of Notre Dame Press, 1999), p. 1.

2 B. Wannenwetsch, 'Luther's Morat Theology', in Donald K. McKim (ed.), *The Cambridge Companion to Martin Luther* (Cambridge: Cambridge University Press, 2003), pp. 120–36.

3 Quoted in J. Summit, *Lost Property: The Woman Writer and English Literary History, 1380–1589* (Chicago, IL: University of Chicago Press, 2000).

4 William Blake, 'Auguries of Innocence', in Geoffrey Keynes (ed.), *Complete Writings* (London: Oxford University Press, 1969), p. 431.

5 Marion Glascoe, *English Medieval Mystics: Games of Faith* (London: Longman, 1993), p. 2.

6 Julian of Norwich, *Revelations of Divine Love* (John Skinner, trans.) (New York: Doubleday, 1996).

7 Sister Elizabeth Ruth Obbard, *Julian: A Woman in Transition* (Annual Julian Lecture, Norwich, 2000), p. 1.

8 Grace M. Jantzen, *Julian of Norwich: Mystic and Theologian* (2nd edn, London: SPCK, 2000), p. 28.

9 *Ancrene Wisse: Guide for Anchoresses* (Hugh White, trans.) (Harmondsworth: Penguin, 1993), p. 66.

10 *Ancrene Wisse*, p. 27.

11 Father John Julian, *The Complete Julian of Norwich* (3rd edn, Brewster, MA: Paraclete Press, 2011), pp. 23–7.

2 Julian's life and times

1 Carole Rawcliffe and Richard Wilson (eds), *Medieval Norwich* (London: Continuum, 2004).

2 Father John Julian, *The Complete Julian of Norwich* (3rd edn, Brewster, MA: Paraclete Press, 2011), p. 30.

3 *The Book of Margery Kempe* (B. A. Windeatt, trans.) (London: Penguin, 1994), p. 77.

4 Father John Julian, *Complete Julian*, p. 385.

5 Rowan Williams, *The Anti-Theology of Julian of Norwich* (The 34th Annual Julian Lecture, 2014), p. 1.

3 Themes in *Revelations of Divine Love*

1 Grace M. Jantzen, *Julian of Norwich: Mystic and Theologian* (2nd edn, London: SPCK, 2000), p. 40.

2 *Ancrene Wisse: Guide for Anchoresses* (Hugh White, trans.) (Harmondsworth: Penguin, 1993), p. 193.

3 Cate Gunn, *Ancrene Wisse: From Pastoral Literature to Vernacular Spirituality* (Cardiff: University of Wales Press, 2008), p. 59.

4 Walter Hilton, *The Scale of Perfection* (Dom Gerard Sitwell, trans.) (London: Burns & Oates, 1953), p. 230.

5 Father John Julian, *The Complete Julian of Norwich* (3rd edn, Brewster, MA: Paraclete Press, 2011), p. 402.

6 Sarah McNamer, 'The Exploratory Image: God as Mother in Julian of Norwich's *Revelations of Divine Love*', *Mystics Quarterly*, 15 (1), 1989, p. 26.

7 McNamer, 'Exploratory Image', pp. 21–28.

8 Jane Chance, 'Heresy and Heterodoxy: The Feminized Trinities of Marguerite Porete and Julian of Norwich', in Catherine Innes-Parker and Naoë Kukita Yoshikawa (eds), *Anchoritism in*

the Middle Ages: Texts and Traditions (Cardiff: University of Wales Press, 2013), pp. 61–82, esp. p. 68.

9 Jantzen, *Julian of Norwich,* p. viii.

10 Jantzen, *Julian of Norwich,* p. 167.

11 Denys Turner, '"Sin is behovely" in Julian of Norwich's *Revelations of Divine Love*', *Modern Theology,* 20 (3), 2004, pp. 407–22.

12 Carmel Bendon Davis, *Mysticism and Space: Space and Spaciality in the Works of Richard Rolle,* The Cloud of Unknowing Author, *and Julian of Norwich* (Washington, DC: Catholic University of America Press, 2008), p. 1.

13 'Chris Hadfield meets Randall Munroe', in the column 'Talk to Me: A Conversation Special', *The Guardian,* 28 November, 2015.

14 *The Cloud of Unknowing,* Chapter 36; Walter Hilton, *The Scale of Perfection,* Chapter 24.

15 Aldous Huxley, *The Perennial Philosophy* (London: Chatto & Windus, 1946), p. 1.

4 A brief history of *Revelations of Divine Love*

1 Cristina Maria Cervona, 'The "Soule" Crux in Julian of Norwich's *A Revelation of Love*', *The Review of English Studies,* 55 (219), April 2004, pp. 151–6.

2 Mary Lou Shea, *Medieval Women on Sin and Salvation: Hadewijch of Antwerp, Beatrice of Nazareth, Margaret Ebner and Julian of Norwich,* American University Studies VII, Vol. 304 (New York: Peter Lang Publications, 2010), p. 1.

3 Umberto Eco, *Baudolino* (William Weaver, trans.) (London: Vintage Books, 2013), p. 434.

4 Thomas Merton, *Seeds of Destruction* (New York: Farrar, Straus & Giroux, 1963), pp. 274–5.

5 Personal communication.

6 Personal communication.

Further reading

This book is intended as a brief introduction to Julian of Norwich and her legacy. It is founded on the research of many more detailed articles and books, which probe deeper into almost every facet of Julian's life and work. By necessity I have had to draw out the ideas and information that most clearly summarize the importance of reading Julian today. This book is by no means exhaustive, and I would guide the interested reader towards these works for further reading.

Note: Quotations throughout are from Barry Windeatt's translation, *Julian of Norwich: Revelations of Divine Love* (Oxford: Oxford University Press, 2015).

Ancrene Wisse: Guide for Anchoresses, trans. Hugh White (Harmondsworth: Penguin, 1993).

Bauerschmidt, Frederick Christian, *Julian of Norwich and the Mystical Body Politic of Christ* (Notre Dame, IN: University of Notre Dame Press, 1999).

Blake, William (ed.), Geoffrey Keynes, *Complete Writings* (London: Oxford University Press, 1969).

The Book of Margery Kempe, trans. B. A. Windeatt (London: Penguin, 1994).

Cervona, Cristina Maria, 'The "Soule" Crux in Julian of Norwich's *A Revelation of Love*', *The Review of English Studies*, 55 (219), April 2004.

Chance, Jane, 'Heresy and Heterodoxy: The Feminized Trinities of Marguerite Porete and Julian of Norwich', in Catherine Innes-Parker and Naoë Kukita Yoshikawa (eds), *Anchoritism in the Middle Ages: Texts and Traditions* (Cardiff: University of Wales Press, 2013).

Collett, Barry, *Late Medieval Englishwomen: Julian of Norwich, Margery Kempe, and Juliana Berners* (Aldershot: Ashgate, 2006).

Further reading

Daffern, Adrian, *The Cross and Julian of Norwich* (Nottingham: Grove Books, 1993).

Davis, Carmel Bendon, *Mysticism and Space: Space and Spaciality in the Works of Richard Rolle,* The Cloud of Unknowing *author, and Julian of Norwich* (Washington, DC: Catholic University of America Press, 2008).

Eco, Umberto, *Baudolino,* trans. William Weaver (London: Vintage Books, 2013).

Fanous, Samuel and Gillespie, Vincent, *The Cambridge Companion to Medieval English Mysticism* (Cambridge: Cambridge University Press, 2012).

Gillespie, Vincent and Powell, Susan, *A Companion to the Early Printed Book in Britain: 1476–1558* (Cambridge: D. S. Brewer, 2014).

Glascoe, Marion, *English Medieval Mystics: Games of Faith* (London: Longman, 1993).

Gunn, Cate, *Ancrene Wisse: From Pastoral Literature to Vernacular Spirituality* (Cardiff: University of Wales, 2008).

Hilton, Walter, *The Scale of Perfection,* trans. Dom Gerard Sitwell (London: Burns & Oates, 1953).

Huxley, Aldous, *The Perennial Philosophy* (London: Chatto & Windus, 1946).

Jantzen, Grace M., *Julian of Norwich: Mystic and Theologian,* 2nd edn (London: SPCK, 2000).

Julian of Norwich, *Revelations of Love,* trans. John Skinner (New York: Doubleday, 1996).

Julian, Father John, *The Complete Julian of Norwich,* 3rd edn (Brewster, MA: Paraclete Press, 2011).

McNamer, Sarah, 'The Exploratory Image: God as Mother in Julian of Norwich's *Revelations of Divine Love*', *Mystics Quarterly*, 15 (1), 1989.

Magill, Kevin J., *Julian of Norwich: Mystic or Visionary?* (Abingdon: Routledge, 2006).

Manton, Karen, and Muir, Lynne, *The Gift of Julian of Norwich* (Leominster: Gracewing, 2005).

Obbard, Sister Elizabeth Ruth, *Julian: A Woman in Transition* (Annual Julian Lecture, Norwich, 2000).

Rawcliffe, Carole and Wilson, Richard (eds), *Medieval Norwich* (London: Continuum, 2004).

Sayer, Frank Dale, *Julian and her Norwich: Commemorative Essays and Handbook to the Exhibition 'Revelations of Divine Love'* (Julian of Norwich 1973 Celebration Committee, 1973).

Shea, Mary Lou, *Medieval Women on Sin and Salvation: Hadewijch of Antwerp, Beatrice of Nazareth, Margaret Ebner and Julian of Norwich*, American University Studies VII, Vol. 304 (New York: Peter Lang Publications, 2010).

Thorne, Brian, *Julian of Norwich: Counsellor for Our Age* (London: Guild of Pastoral Psychology, 1999).

Turner, Denys, '"Sin is behovely" in Julian of Norwich's *Revelations of Divine Love*', *Modern Theology*, 20 (3), 2004.

Upjohn, Sheila, *All Shall be Well: Daily Readings from Julian of Norwich* (London: Darton, Longman & Todd, 1992).

Williams, Rowan, *The Anti-Theology of Julian of Norwich* (The 34th Annual Julian Lecture, 2014).

Index

adulterers 56
'all shall be well' 59, 63
  see also hope; optimism
anchoresses 5, 10, 15
  asceticism (bodily) 38
  life of 11–12, 13
  rites of enclosure 13
Ancrene Wisse 10–11, 54–5, 62
Anselm of Canterbury 50
Aquinas, Thomas 35
asceticism (bodily) 37–8
Augustine of Hippo 35

Ball, John 25
Battle of North Walsham 26
Beguines 17–18
  see also Marie of Oignies
'behovely' 4, 58
  see also sin: as 'behovely'
Bernard of Clairvaux 50
Black Death (1348–9) 23–4,
  42
blindness of humanity 46
block printing 30
blood of Christ 43–5
bodily visions 8
Book of Margery Kempe, The
  (Kempe) 19, 20–1
bride of Christ, a 54–5
Bridget of Sweden, St 6

Cambrai nuns 76–7, 78–80
Carrow Abbey 14, 15, 34

Christ
  connecting with 41
  as Mother 52
  suffering 40–1
  see also cross of Christ; crucifix
church leadership 26–7
churches, decoration 42
cloth industry 18
Cloud of Unknowing, The author
  7, 32, 37, 44, 46, 66
Collins, Henry 80–1
compassion 48
confession 57
Crecy, Serenus de 78
crime and punishment 47
  see also sin
cross of Christ
  in art 42
  blood 43–5
  as comfort 40
crown of thorns 40, 41
crucifix 40–1, 42–3
crusades 27

Dante Alighieri: *Divine Comedy*
  56
desire 52–5
  sexual 54–5
Despenser, Henry (Bishop of
  Norwich) 25–6, 27, 38
Despenser Retable (Norwich
  Cathedral) 42
dialects 4

Index

Divine Comedy (Dante) 56
divine judgement 47
'doom paintings' 47, 56

Eco, Umberto: *Baudolino* 83
Edward III 15, 26
Einstein, Albert, on mystical
    experiences 64
Emund, Thomas 18
enclosure (religious), rites of 13
English, writings in 7–9, 28
equality before God 46
Erpingham, Sir Thomas 14–15
eschatology 56–7
executions 29
existentialism 66–7

fasting 37–8
femininity 49–50
feudal system 24
Fonds Anglais No. 40 (P) 77–8
forgiveness 48
free will 58
French Revolution 79
friaries 17

ghostly visions 8
Gillespie, Vincent 84
God
    encounters with 8
    Julian's concept 46, 50
    as Mother 9, 50–2
    source of love 46
Great Western Schism 26–7
guilds 17

Hadfield, Chris 65
hagiography 41

hazelnut analogy 58, 65
heaven 57
hell 57
heresy 29, 74
Heresy Trials 29
hermits 10
Hildegard of Bingen 6
Hilton, Walter 7, 44, 46, 51, 66
hope 25, 31–2, 63–4
Howard, Richard 42
Hundred Years War 26
Huxley, Aldous 68–9

indulgences 56
inner strength 62–4
intellectual enlightenment 8

John of Beverley, St 60–1
Julian of Erpingham 14–16
Julian of Norwich
    audience written for 46
    becoming anchoress 12–13
    contact with populace of
        Norwich 19
    formal education 32–4, 36
    God, concept of 46, 50
    her cell 18–19
    identity 14–16
    images of 23
    influences on writing 31–2
    Lollard sympathies 29–30
    message of hope 31–2
    mystical experiences 38–40
    near-death experience 38–40,
        53
    philosophical niche 65–9
    revelations 3, 5, 37
    sin, concept of 57–62

Index

temperament 38
theology 35–6
unique writing style 34–5
use of imagery 44–5
justice 47–9
justice system, in medieval society 47

Kempe, Margery 6, 7, 53, 55
    accused of Lollardy 29
    Book of Margery Kempe, The 19, 20–1
    dictates to scribe 34
    heretic 21
    mysticism 20
    notoriety 22
    visiting Julian 20–1
    as writer 21–2, 23
Kierkegaard, Søren 66

Ladder of Perfection 51, 61, 63, 66
languages 33
Last Judgement 56
Latin 33
Lawrence, St 41
liars 56
Litster, Geoffrey 25
literacy rates 33
Lollard's Pit 29
Lollardy 22, 28–9, 57
Long Text 4–5
    Christ as Mother 52
    concept of femininity 50
    manuscripts 77–8
    and sin 60
lord and servant parable 47–9, 51

love 45–6, 49
    in relation to sin and punishment 59–60
    unconditional 51
    see also mercy

macabre, society's fixation with 41
manuscripts of *Revelations* 77–8, 79–80
Marie of Oignies 6
    see also Beguines
medieval society 10–11, 17–18, 26
    intellectual and spiritual structure 31
    justice system 47
    theological methods 8–9
    views on mortality 39–40
mercy 47–9
    see also love
Merton, Thomas 84
Middle English 3–4, 52, 81
monasteries 17
More, Gertrude 76–7
mortality, medieval views 39–40
mortification 6
Mother God 9, 50–2
MS Sloane 2499 (S1) 77–8, 82
MS Sloane 3705 (S2) 77
mystical experiences 8–9, 37
    of Julian 38–40
    temporal representation 64–6
    through physical punishment 37–8
    see also revelations

Index

mystical texts 6–7, 75–6
  audiences written for 46
mysticism 5–8
mystics, contemporary 6–8

Norwich 17–19, 24, 33
Norwich Cathedral 17

optimism 25, 63–4

patronage 56
Peasants' Revolt (1381) 25, 28
perennialism 67–9
perfection, striving for 51, 61,
  63, 66
persecution 22
philosophical schools 66–9
physical punishment, mystical
  experiences through 37–8
plagues 23–5
political upheaval 24
Porynlond, Richard 42
prayer nuts 58–9
printing press, invention 30–1
Protestant Reformation (English)
  3–4, 75–6
purgatory 56–7

Reed, Richard 18
religious groups 17–18
religious imagery 44–5
religious upheaval 26–7
religious withdrawal 10–11, 12
revelations 3, 5, 37, 38–40
Revelations of Divine Love
  and Cambrai nuns 76–7
  description 9

distribution 74–5, 78
  Long Text 4–5
  modern criticism 84
  motherly tone 15
  printed history 78–9, 80–2
  reception in print 3–4
  relevance today 82–5
  self-scribed by Julian 34
  Short Text 4–5
  as spiritual biography 3
  survival of texts 73
Richard II 25
Rolle, Richard 7, 10, 32, 35, 46,
  66

Sara, Julian's maid 18
sexual desires 54–5
Short Text 4–5
  concept of femininity 49
  and sin 60
sin
  as 'behovely' 58–9, 61–2
  and free will 58
  Julian's concept 57–62
  and punishment 56–7
solitaries 10
spirituality 36
Stanbrook Abbey 76–7, 82
Sudbury, Simon 25
suffering 62–4
summum bonum 68–9

theology, medieval methods
  8–9
trade, medieval society 17, 26
transcendentalism 67
transi tombs 41–2

Index

Tyler, Wat 25
tympanum, Sainte Foy 56

unconditional love 51
usurers 56

vernacular, use of 7–9, 28
Virgin Mary 51–2
visions 3, 5, 37, 38–40

Warrack, Grace 81–2
Williams, Rowan 84
womb imagery 50–1
women
    role in society 54, 81, 84
    role in theological
        enlightenment 8–9
    wise 32
Wycliffe, John 28–9